T0213622

Lecture Notes
in Business Information Processing   **286**

Series Editors

Wil M.P. van der Aalst
  Eindhoven Technical University, Eindhoven, The Netherlands
John Mylopoulos
  University of Trento, Trento, Italy
Michael Rosemann
  Queensland University of Technology, Brisbane, QLD, Australia
Michael J. Shaw
  University of Illinois, Urbana-Champaign, IL, USA
Clemens Szyperski
  Microsoft Research, Redmond, WA, USA

More information about this series at http://www.springer.com/series/7911

Andreas Metzger · Anne Persson (Eds.)

Advanced Information Systems Engineering Workshops

CAiSE 2017 International Workshops
Essen, Germany, June 12–16, 2017
Proceedings

 Springer

Editors
Andreas Metzger
Universität Duisburg-Essen
Essen
Germany

Anne Persson
University of Skövde
Skövde
Sweden

ISSN 1865-1348   ISSN 1865-1356 (electronic)
Lecture Notes in Business Information Processing
ISBN 978-3-319-60047-5   ISBN 978-3-319-60048-2 (eBook)
DOI 10.1007/978-3-319-60048-2

Library of Congress Control Number: 2017943010

Printed on acid-free paper

This Springer imprint is published by Springer Nature
The registered company is Springer International Publishing AG
The registered company address is: Gewerbestrasse 11, 6330 Cham, Switzerland

Preface

The Conference on Advanced Information Systems Engineering (CAiSE) has a long tradition of hosting thematic workshops around information systems topics. CAiSE workshops provide ample room for discussion of recent developments as well as new and emerging ideas. The 29th CAiSE was held in Essen, Germany, during June 12–16, 2017 under the theme "Digital Connected World – Informed, Disruptive Business Transformation."

We received nine workshop proposals for CAiSE 2017, of which we selected five workshops after careful consideration, based on maturity and quality, providing a balanced set of events. Two kinds of workshops were selected: (1) paper-oriented workshops, which concentrate on presentations of accepted papers with associated discussions; (2) discussion-oriented workshops, which have an emphasis on discussions facilitated by paper presentations.

This volume contains the proceedings of the following three workshops of CAiSE 2017 (in alphabetical order):

- The 4th International Workshop on Advances in Services Design Based on the Notion of Capability (ASDENCA)
- The 5th International Workshop on Cognitive Aspects of Information Systems Engineering (COGNISE)
- The First International Workshop on Teaching for Smart Information Systems – Smart Information Systems for Teaching (T4SIS4T), which took place as a dedicated session under the umbrella of the COGNISE workshop

In addition, the following two workshops took place at CAiSE 2017:

- The 13th International Workshop on Enterprise and Organizational Modeling and Simulation (EOMAS), which published its proceedings in a separate LNBIP volume
- The Third International Workshop on Socio-Technical Perspective in IS Development (STPIS), which published its proceedings in the CEUR Workshop proceedings series

Each workshop adhered to the CAiSE 2017 submission and acceptance guidelines. The paper acceptance rate for the workshops included in these proceedings was approximately 41%.

As workshop chairs of CAiSE 2017, we would like to express our gratitude to the workshop organizers and the Program Committee members of the workshops for their valuable contributions.

April 2017

Andreas Metzger
Anne Persson

4th International Workshop on Advances in Service Design Based on the Notion of Capability - ASDENCA

Preface

Lately, the notion of capability is gaining much attention within the field of information systems engineering thanks to a number of factors: the notion directs business investment focus, it can be used as a baseline for business planning, and it leads directly to service specification and design. Historically, it has been examined in economics, sociology, and management science. More recently, it has been considered in the context of business-IT alignment, in the specification and design of services using business planning as the baseline.

Capability is commonly seen as an ability or capacity for a company to deliver value, either to customers or to shareholders, right beneath the business strategy. It consists of three major components: business processes, people, and physical assets.

Thus it is as an abstraction away from the specifics of how (process), who (agent), and why (goals), i.e., with a focus on results and benefits. At the same time, capability should allow for fairly straightforward integrations with the aforementioned established bodies of knowledge and practices, such as goals (through "goal fulfilment"), processes (through "modelling"), and services (through "servicing").

The idea for the ASDENCA workshop came from the academic and industrial community gathered during the EU/FP7 project "CaaS." In its fourth year, ASDENCA was concerned with discussing today's important IS engineering problems that could be solved by achieving capability for embodying software solutions capturing changes in business contexts to support sustainable run-time management of the business.

The Program Committee selected four high-quality papers for presentation at the workshop, which are included in the CAiSE 2017 Workshops proceedings volume.

We owe special thanks to the workshop chairs of CAiSE 2017 for supporting the ASDENCA workshop, as well as for providing us with the facilities to publicize it. We also thank the Program Committee for providing valuable and timely reviews of the submitted papers.

April 2017

Jelena Zdravkovic
Oscar Pastor
Peri Loucopoulos

ASDENCA Organization

Organizing Committee

Jelena Zdravkovic   Stockholm University, Sweden
Pericles Loucopoulos   University of Manchester, UK
Oscar Pastor   University of Valencia, Spain

Program Committee

Mohhamad Danesh, Canada
Janis Grabis, Latvia
Giancarlo Guizzardi, Brazil
Martin Henkel, Sweden
Amin Jalali, Sweden
Janis Kampars, Latvia
Dimitris Karagiannis, Austria
Marite Kirikova, Latvia
Raimundas Matulevicius, Estonia
Andreas Opdahl, Norway

Ilias Petroounias, UK
Jolita Ralyte, Switzerland
Gil Regev, Switzerland
Kurt Sandkuhl, Germany
Pnina Soffer, Israel
Janis Stirna, Sweden
Francisco Valverde, Spain
Hans Weigand, The Netherlands
Eric Yu, Canada

5th International Workshop on Cognitive Aspects of Information Systems Engineering – COGNISE

Preface

Cognitive aspects of software and information systems engineering have received increasing attention in the literature and at conferences in recent years, acknowledging that these aspects are as important as the technical ones, which have traditionally been at the center of attention. This workshop serves as a stage for new research and lively discussions on this topic, involving both academics and practitioners.

The goal of this workshop is to provide a better understanding and more appropriate support of the cognitive processes and challenges practitioners experience when performing information systems development activities. Understanding the challenges and needs, offering educational programs, as well as developing supporting tools and notations may be enhanced for a better fit to our natural cognition, leading to a better performance of engineers and higher system quality. This year the workshop included an additional contemporary topic: virtual and augmented reality systems and the new challenges these cutting-edge technologies present to their developers.

The workshop aims to bring together researchers from different communities— such as requirements engineering, software architecture, modeling, design and programming, and information systems education— who share an interest in cognitive aspects, for identifying the cognitive challenges in the diverse development-related activities and for proposing relevant solutions.

The fifth edition of this workshop, held in Essen on June 13, 2017, was organized in conjunction with the 29th International Conference on Advanced Information Systems Engineering (CAiSE 2017). This edition attracted 11 international submissions. Each paper was reviewed by three members of the Program Committee. Of these submissions, five papers were accepted for inclusion in the proceedings (45%). The papers presented at the workshop provide a mix of novel research ideas, showcasing full research, research in progress, or research plans. In addition, the workshop hosted two keynote speeches, one presenting the newly added topic of virtual and augmented reality, discussing the state of the art in industry, and the other presenting a recently completed systematic literature review on the comprehension of process models. Extended abstracts of these keynote speeches are included in the proceedings.

We hope that the reader will find this selection of papers useful and they will be informed and inspired by new ideas in the area of cognitive aspects of information systems engineering. We look forward to future editions of the COGNISE workshop following the five editions we have had to date.

April 2017

Irit Hadar
Irene Vanderfeesten
Barbara Weber

COGNISE Organization

Organizing Committee

Irit Hadar	University of Haifa, Israel
Irene Vanderfeesten	Eindhoven University of Technology
Barbara Weber	Technical University of Denmark and University of Innsbruck, Austria

Program Committee

Banu Aysolmaz	VU University of Amsterdam, The Netherlands
Daniel M. Berry	University of Waterloo, Canada
Kathrin Figl	WU Vienna, Austria
Stijn Hoppenbrouwers	HAN University of Applied Sciences, Arnhem, and Radboud University of Nijmegen, The Netherlands
Marta Indulska	University of Queensland, Australia
Joel Lanir	University of Haifa, Israel
Meira Levy	Shenkar College of Engineering and Design, Israel
Jonas Bulegon Gassen	WU Vienna, Austria
Jeffrey Parsons	Memorial University, Canada
Geert Poels	Ghent University, Belgium
Maryam Razavian	Eindhoven University of Technology, The Netherlands
Alexander Serebrenik	Eindhoven University of Technology, The Netherlands
Pnina Soffer	University of Haifa, Israel
Dirk van der Linden	University of Haifa, Israel
Anna Zamansky	University of Haifa, Israel

First International Workshop on Teaching for Smart Information Systems - Smart Information Systems for Teaching - T4SIS4T

Preface

As information technology and information systems have increasingly pervaded organizations and all aspects of our lives, gaining an in-depth understanding of information systems is becoming increasingly difficult. As a result, teaching information system subjects becomes very challenging: Our students need to gain a deeper understanding of the complexity of service-based systems while being able to assess the impact of such systems on the many aspects of organizations and personal life. At the same time, "smart" technologies such as machine learning as well as context awareness and adaptation attempt to raise the level of intelligence of information systems. However, leveraging the possibilities of smart technologies for "digital" teaching is far from evident. T4SIS4T aimed to foster a discussion on two main topics. The first is innovative approaches to teach complex information systems subjects. The second is how to leverage the power of information technology to create smart learning environments that improve the teaching and learning of complex subjects through, e.g., awareness of and adaptation to learning subject, learner profile, learner behavior, etc.

The first edition of this workshop accepted two papers out of five submissions. The paper of M. Levy addresses the first topic. The development of smart information systems requires design processes that involve multidisciplinary perspectives. Smart information systems education should therefore incorporate teaching approaches in which students can gain experiences in working effectively in multidisciplinary teams. The paper of M. Levy presents insights from the organization of multidisciplinary teaching events that aim at developing design thinking in multidisciplinary learning teams. The second paper addresses the second topic. S. Oppl and S. Hoppenbrouwers designed and implemented a Web-based instrument that supports learning about modeling concepts via participatory simulation to support experiential learning.

We would like to thank all the people who contributed to the realization of the first T4SIS4T workshop: the authors who submitted their interesting papers, the reviewers who ensured the quality of the review process and provided the authors with constructive feedback, and the CAiSE Workshop organizers (Andreas Metzger and Anne Persson) for their valuable support.

April 2017

Monique Snoeck
Jochen De Weerdt
Estefanía Serral Asensio
Irit Hadar
Geraldine Clarebout

T4SIS4T Organization

Organizing Committee

Monique Snoeck	KU Leuven, Belgium
Jochen De Weerdt	KU Leuven, Belgium
Estefanía Serral Asensio	KU Leuven, Belgium
Irit Hadar	University of Haifa, Israel
Geraldine Clarebout	Maastricht University, The Netherlands

Program Committee

Amir Tomer	Kinneret Academic College, Israel
Anna Zamansky	University of Haifa, Israel
Beatriz Marín	Universidad Diego Portales, Chile
Dirk van der Linden	University of Haifa, Israel
Jan Claes	UGent, Belgium
Jeroen Donkers	Maastricht University, The Netherlands
Kathrin Figl	WU, Austria
Kirsty Kitto	QUT, Australia
Lars Bollen	UTwente, The Netherlands
Meira Levy	Shenkar College of Engineering and Design, Israel
Michał Śmiałek	Warsaw University of Technology, Poland
Oscar Pastor	Universidad Politécnica de Valencia, Spain
Sofia Sherman	Waterloo University, Canada
Stijn Hoppenbrouwers	Radboud University, The Netherlands
Stefaan Ternier	Open University, The Netherlands
Stelios Asteriadis	Maastricht University, The Netherlands
Suriadi Suriadi	QUT, Australia

Keynote Abstracts

Cognitive Augmented and Mixed Reality: A New Era of Interaction

Ethan Hadar

IBM Research Labs, Haifa, Israel
Ethan@il.ibm.com

Keywords: Augmented Reality • Users Interactions

This talk will examine the implications of cognitive Augmented and Mixed Reality (AR/MR) technologies on information systems engineering and their effect on personalized, immersive computing. AR/MR technologies facilitate interactions with users involving enhanced 3D vision, spatial hearing, hands and arms gestures, and vocal interactions, as well as controlling information flow of IoT devices monitoring and controlling the physical surrounding environment. Given the complexity of these personalized immersive interactions, a change is needed in information systems engineering, particularly in requirements engineering and quality assurance practices.

Requirements gathering and validation of users' experience implies that development engineers need to experience, understand, and use these new AR/MR modes of interactions. One wonders how would engineers perform activities such as shadowing, recording and analyzing users' actions, fully understand gestures and gazing intent, factoring eyesight limitations, depth perceptions, and more.

Virtual Reality (VR) uses comprehensive digital environment devices and digital cues. However, AR/MR require hands-free for interacting with real world environment in which there are no pointers nor cues. Repeated VR digital world can track and monitor user's actions and derive usability statistics. Real environments behave according to the laws of nature and users' personalized parameters in addition to the interacted digital information overlay. AR and MR are meant for augmenting users' eyesight, audio, gestures and cognitive collaboration with the IT systems, whilst developers are required to create generic software solutions that abstracts these cognitive interactions as well as encapsulate hardware complexity such as the camera field-of-view versus the person, or wearables' comfort levels.

How should requirements engineering and quality assurance disciplines evolve to assist developers in understanding how and what needs to be improved, added, or removed in AR/MR driven systems? How can we perform agile enhancements in UX and UI, normalize, relate and transform the input provided from field experience, to practical actions? How should the development environment look like when dealing with AR/MR systems? What will be the new form of unit testing?

There is a need for research to answer these questions.

Examples will be given from different domains such as industrial support and maintenance, automotive and aerospace manufacturing, and more.

Why Are Process Models Hard to Understand?

Kathrin Figl ⬤

Institute for Information Systems and New Media, Vienna University
of Economics and Business, Vienna, Austria
kathrin.figl@wu.ac.at

Even the most brilliant process model would not be of any use if no one could understand it. A basic precondition for a model's usefulness in practice is that it is comprehensible.

This keynote covers the emerging field of empirical research in to the comprehensibility of process models. It gives an overview of the factors that influence comprehension based on a recent, thorough literature review [1]. This included forty empirical studies that measured the objective comprehension of process models and seven studies that measured subjective comprehension and user preferences. Table 1 *presents an overview of all the categories of influencing factors investigated in these studies.* This keynote presents and discusses all the main, relevant effects on model comprehension.

Table 1. Factors influencing process model comprehension.

Main categories	Exemplary subcategories
Presentation medium	Paper versus computer
Notation	Representation paradigm (e.g., text versus model, animation), primary notation (e.g., BPMN), notational characteristics
Secondary notation	Decomposition, highlighting of control blocks, layout
Label	Label design, naming conventions
Model characteristics	Size measures, modularity, structuredness, gateway interplay
Task	Wording of comprehension tasks
User	Domain knowledge, modeling knowledge

Overall, the literature review yielded cumulative evidence for a variety of variables related to process model comprehension while it also identified research gaps. Regarding research methods, future work should adopt eye-tracking more often as it can detect mental effort variations more precisely than traditional multiple-choice tasks used to measure comprehension.

Taken together, this keynote provides researchers with an update of current empirical research, contrasts it to existing modeling guidelines, and contributes to the vibrant stream of research in to process model comprehension.

Reference

1. Figl, K.: Comprehension of procedural visual business process models. Bus. Inf. Syst. Eng. **59**, 41–67 (2017)

Contents

T4SIS4T – Teaching for Smart Information Systems – Smart Information

ASDENCA 2017 – Advances in Services Design Based on the Notion of Capability

Design of Vehicle Routing Capability

Jānis Grabis[1(✉)], Jānis Kampars[1], Žanis Bondars[1], and Ēriks Dobelis[2]

[1] Institute of Information Technology, Riga Technical University, Kalku 1, Riga, Latvia
{grabis,janis.kampars,zanis.bondars}@rtu.lv
[2] LLC PricewaterhouseCoopers, Kr. Valdemara 21-21, Riga, Latvia
eriks.dobelis@lv.pwc.com

Abstract. Vehicle routing deals with assigning a set of vehicles to service geographically distributed customers. Modern information technologies such as sensing and cloud computing technologies have significantly affected the way this problem is addressed. It is a computationally intensive and context-aware multi-objective decision-making problem. The Capability Driven Development is suitable for tackling that kind of problems. It is goal-oriented, captures decision-making context and allows to decouple computationally intensive decision-making logics from the core application. This paper describes development of the vehicle routing capability model. This model is intended for usage by companies providing vehicle routing as a service to multiple providers of logistical services. It allows customization of vehicle routing solutions of individual consumers on the basis of the common reference model. The common reference model also serves as a basis for accumulating vehicle routing knowledge.

Keywords: Capability · Adaptation · Run-time · Context · Vehicle routing

1 Introduction

Services have become one of the prevalent ways of delivering information technology solutions to customers [1]. Multi-tenancy is one of the key principles of service-orientation [2] and the same services are provided to a diverse group of customers experiencing their own unique operating circumstances. The Capability Driven Development (CDD) [3, 4] has been proposed as an approach for designing and delivering services able to provide expected performance in various contextual situations. This approach assumes that in order to achieve that a service provider must possess a service delivery capability. This capability explicitly defines service delivery goals, identifies contextual elements affecting service delivery and specifies service adaptation mechanisms dealing with contextual changes and non-performance.

This paper focuses on a vehicle routing problem [5] what is on the typical managerial problems faced by many companies, and the problem solving is significantly affected by context [6]. It deals with finding a set of routes served by multiple vehicles that jointly traverse a number of customers. The vehicle routing decision-making problem also must be addressed as a part of the overall fleet management information system [7, 8].

It is assumed that vehicle routing service is provided by a company and it is used by several logistics service providers who operate a fleet of vehicles and service their

© Springer International Publishing AG 2017
A. Metzger and A. Persson (Eds.): CAiSE 2017 Workshops, LNBIP 286, pp. 3–13, 2017.
DOI: 10.1007/978-3-319-60048-2_1

customers. The routing service is provided on the basis of the common vehicle routing capability possessed by the company. The capability supports customization of the service for the customers and enables knowledge sharing, especially, sharing of contextual information.

The objective of this paper is to develop the vehicle routing capability and to illustrate its application. The vehicle routing capability is developed and delivered following the CDD methodology. Particular attention is devoted to describing capability delivery adjustments, which allow tailoring the service for needs of individual service consumers and adaption of the service depending on its performance and changes in context.

The rest of the paper is organized as follows. Section 1 recaps main concepts of the CDD methodology. The routing problem from the service provider perspective is described in Sect. 3. The routing capability is developed in Sect. 4. That includes definition of routing adjustments. Capability delivery is discussed in Sect. 5. Section 6 concludes.

2 Background

Capabilities are designed on the basis of the capability meta-model [3] following guidelines of the CDD methodology. The CDD methodology also defines activities performed during capability delivery.

2.1 Capability Modeling

The capability model defines service provider's ability and capacity to deliver an appropriate solution to clients facing specific circumstances. Figure 1 shows a simplified overview of the key elements used in capability modeling. Goals are business objectives the capability allows to achieve. They are measured by KPI. The capability is designed for delivery in a specific context as defined using context elements. The context elements name factors affecting the capability delivery while context situations refer to combinations of context element values. The process element specifies a capability delivery solution.

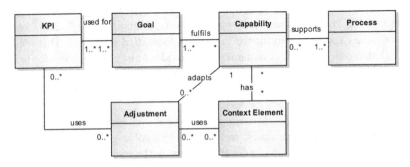

Fig. 1. Key concepts of capability modeling

In order to ensure that capability is delivered as expected in different contextual situations, adjustments are used to adapt capability delivery [9]. The adjustments take context data and KPI as input and evaluate potential changes in capability delivery. They are also used to implement complex context-dependent decision-making logics.

2.2 Capability Design and Delivery

The capability development is performed according to the CDD methodology. Its main features are:

- Enterprise modelling phase, which defines information about the digital enterprise necessary to specify requirements for development of capable information systems. It allows involving business people in information system development;
- Design phase, where the capable information systems is designed on the basis of the existing knowledge in a model-driven manner;
- Delivery phase, where the capable information system is executed, monitored and adjusted to changes in the operating environment if necessary;
- Feedback phase, where the system delivery experiences are accumulated and changes in the design are requested.

The capability model is developed during the design phases. The model is used to configure the capability delivery solution. The adjustments are also implemented during the design phase. The CDD methodology focuses on development of adaptable components of the overall capability deliverer solution. Problem area and case specific engineering methods can be used to develop other components. The delivery phase concerns run-time aspects. In the framework of this paper, the main aspect of capability delivery is execution of capability delivery adjustments. The adjustments are executed in separate container and interact with the other parts of the capability delivery solution through well-defined interfaces.

3 Problem Statement

Vehicle routing deals with finding a set of routes served by multiple vehicles that jointly traverse a number of customers [5]. This paper assumes that there are three parties involved in the vehicle routing problem: (1) vehicle routing service provider addressing data processing and planning needs; (2) logistics service provider operating the fleet of vehicles and servicing customers; and (3) customers requesting logistics services.

A company providing routing services develops and operates a vehicle routing solution for logistics service providers. That includes routing software as a service, accumulation of vehicle routing knowledge, data gathering and decision-making support. The services offered are configured for specific logistics service providers.

A company providing logistics services operates a fleet of vehicles. It receives customer service requests on the periodical basis. The customers should be visited within a specified time window. The vehicles should be routed to serve the customers at minimum cost where the cost can be expressed as a sum of multiple factors. The routes start and end at a depot. The main decision variables are vehicle allocation to customers and vehicle arrival time at the customer. The routing problem is formulated as a mathematical programming model and optimal routes are found by performing route optimization.

The company has multiple vehicles routing objectives including customer services level satisfaction, environmental impact reduction and ensuring a safe working environment. The objectives are measured by a set of KPI. Every KPI has a target value specified by management. The route optimization should be performed to take into account these specific KPI and their deviation from the target value. Actual values of KPI depend upon routing decisions made. The route execution is affected by several case specific context factors such as weather, traffic accidents and calendar events. The context factors are beyond company's control.

Route planning and execution occurs on regular basis. For example, a set of customer requests is received at the beginning of each day, optimal routes are found and customers are visited during the day following these routes. Performance data are accumulated and context data are observed during the route execution. These data are compared with the planned values and deviations are observed. In particular, the actual KPI values are evaluated and compared with those estimated during the route optimization. One of the reasons of potential deviations is that different KPI are mutually contradicting and the right trade-off among the objectives has not been achieved. That can be remedied by changing relative importance of KPI represented by appropriate parameters in the optimization models. The change is performed in an adaptive manner because the right balance is not known in advance.

Similarly, context values are observed and these observations can be used to evaluate relationships among them, decisions-made and performance achieved. This way one can estimate impact of context on performance and this information can be incorporated in the optimization model in an adaptive manner.

4   Routing Capability

The routing capability is designed as a part of collaborative industrial research project with a consulting company. The model is developed to provide a comprehensive view of the vehicle routing problem and it attempts to incorporate all relevant concepts identified by means of literature review and interviews with logistics service providers.

4.1   Capability Model

The capability model developed is shown in Fig. 2. According to the CDD methodology, it consists of three main parts: (1) goal; (2) context; and (3) service delivery solution. These parts of the model were developed in sequence. The vehicle routing problem is a multi-objective problem [10] as manifested by several goals identified as driving routing decisions (the goals are represented by a shaded box with rounded corners and are identified and name and suffix "Gl"). Achievement of the goals is measured by KPI and every KPI also has its target value. The figure shows only a sub-set of goals and their KPI. Sixteen

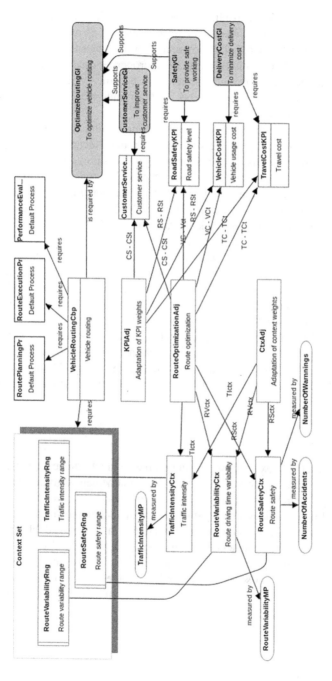

Fig. 2. Vehicle routing capability.

goals were identified in total. All goals area included in the model though only the relevant goals are activated for individual logistics service providers during the capability delivery.

Context elements affecting capability delivery are also identified. The figure shows only a few exemplary context elements and nineteen context elements are identified in total (referenced with suffix "Ctx"). Each context element is measured by one or several measurable properties. Combination of measurable properties used to evaluate a context element can be modified if more suitable data have become available. Different data sources for a measurable property can be used for individual service consumers depending on local data availability.

The context-dependent adaptable part of the vehicle routing solution is represented by three processes: (1) route planning process; (2) route execution process; and (3) performance evaluation process. The route planning process is executed periodically to find travel routes for a given set of customer requests. The route execution concerns actual customer service along the route planned and gathering of feedback information about actual contextual situations experienced and performance achieved. The performance evaluation process uses the feedback information to update parameters of the route planning process.

The capability delivery adaption and decision-making logics is defined in adjustments (identified by suffix "Adj"). The main adjustment is the Route optimization adjustment, which calculates routes to be traversed by vehicles. It takes KPI and context elements as input parameters. It encapsulates the vehicle routing decision-making logics. The routing model implemented in this adjustment is described in Sect. 4.2. This model depends among others upon two sets of parameters, namely, KPI weights and context weights (see Sect. 4.2). Values of these parameters are periodically adapted to steer capability delivery. This adaptive behavior is implemented using KPIAdj and CtxAdj, respectively. CtxAdj takes the context elements as an input while KPIAdj takes KPI as an input.

4.2 Adjustments

Vehicle routing is a complex decision-making problem, which can be expressed mathematically and solved using appropriate methods. A mathematical formulation of the vehicle routing problem in a matrix form is given in Table 1. Its core part is a typical formulation [11] used in many investigations and practical applications. It optimizes routing cost and its main decision-making variable is a binary variable indicating whether a vehicle travels from one client to another. This matrix of decision variables is denoted by $\mathbf{X}$. The main constraints are that each client is visited exactly once, vehicles have finite capacity, customer service time windows, routes start and finish at a depot, if vehicle arrives at a client it also must leave and departure, transit and arrival time dependences.

Table 1. Generic and customizable parts of the routing model.

Core part	Customizable part	
$\min Z = \mathbf{c'X}$	$+\mathbf{v'P}$	(1)
$\mathbf{aX} \leq \mathbf{b}$		(2)
$\mathbf{c} = \mathbf{d}$	$+\mathbf{ctx} \times \mathbf{w}$	(3)
	$\mathbf{KPI}^C(\mathbf{X}) + \mathbf{P} = \mathbf{kpi}^T$	(4)

The vector **c** represents expense of taking a particular path between two clients. In the generic formulation this expense equals to **d**, which represents travel distance. Vectors **a** and **b** are parameters used to specify constraints.

The generic model is augmented by a part representing individual requirements of specific logistics service providers. These specific requirements concern goals and context. The objective function is augmented by adding a term **v'P**, where **P** is a vector of penalties for not meeting company's specific goals and **v** is a vector of weights indicating a relative importance of each goal. A corresponding set of constraints (Eq. 4) is also added to the model. These constraints represent relationships among target values of KPI and values estimated by the model. $\mathbf{kpi}^T$ are target values set by decision-makers and $\mathbf{KPI}^C$ is a KPI value estimated using the routing model. This estimated value depends on the decision variable **X**. The constraint implies that if the target KPI value is not achieved then a positive penalty is added to the objective function. The penalty term in the objective function and the KPI constraint are added according to the goals and their measurements specified in the goal model.

Additionally, constraint Eq. 3 is also modified. The cost of the route is now calculated as a sum of the distance and the weighted impact of context factors (the weight vector **w**). This modification implies that the cost parameters characterize different aspects of the route. For instance, there is a short route where accidents frequently occur; the aggregated cost parameter captures these characteristics. The aggregated cost parameter is defined as c_{ijk} implying that there are k different routes leading from i to j. These different routes are obtained by finding the best path from i to j using different sets of **w**. For instance, one set of **w** favours the shortest path while another set of **w** favours the safest path.

The routing model depends on a number of weighting parameters. The initial values of these parameters are specified in a judgmental manner. Subsequently, they are continuously updated to improve routing performance. The adaption is performed periodically once information about route execution is accumulated in the transportation planning application. Adaptation is also one of the mechanisms used to customize the solution.

5 Sample Routing Results

The vehicle routing solution is implemented on the basis of the capability model and can be used by various logistics service providers. The capability delivery solution is implemented as a web based geographical information system, which includes modules for vehicle routing setup, demand data management, context data management, route planning, route execution and performance evaluation. Some of these models are configured according to the capability model. The vehicle routing setup uses the list of goals, KPI and context elements. The context data management module uses information about measurable properties and establishes binding with case specific data sources. Route planning and performance evaluation modules besides their other functions use route optimization, KPI weights and context weights adaption adjustments to implement the context-aware performance driven logics. The adjustments specified in the capability model are packaged as web services. The respective modules invoke these web services for decision-making purposes.

The routing solution is set-up for two logistics services providers, namely, LSP1 and LSP2. The providers receive client requests on the daily bases and must visit these clients during specified time windows. Both providers have identified that their primary KPI are KPI1) customer service measured as a percentage of the clients served during the specified time windows; KPI2) travel cost calculated as time spent on deliveries times hourly rate; KPI3) vehicle operating cost incurred for every vehicle used on a given day regardless of distance travelled; and KPI4) safety aimed at avoiding traversal of accident prone routes measured by an index characterizing frequency of the accidents. LSP1 also indicates that two major context elements affecting its operations are: CTX1) route variability measured as variation of driving time from day to day; and CTX2) route safety measured as a number of accidents observed for the given route. LSP2 does not consider these context factors significant and does not include them in the model.

Routing is performed for 20 client requests received for a single day. The travel distance and time data are retrieved from OpenStreetMap (https://www.openstreet map.org). The accident data are gathered from a web mapping service. The same client data set is used for LSP1 and LSP2.

Figure 3 illustrates differences between routing results for LSP1 and LSP2. It can be observed that different paths are selected on several occasions. In the case of LSP2, the traveling distance is the only factor used to evaluate cost associated with traveling from one customer to another. LSP1 also took into account other contextual factors resulting leading to a different set of routes what indicates context-dependency in path selection.

The adaption is performed to alter balance among KPI in the objective function. This adaption is invoked periodically using the KPIAdj adjustment as performance data have been accumulated. Five adaption cycles are performed for LSP1. The same set of customer requests is used in all five cycles though different customer requests would be expected in real life situations. Table 2 shows the adaption results. KPI values are reported relative to the target values. Values above one indicate that the KPI target value has been achieved. In the first cycle the set of weights $\mathbf{v}$ has values $(0.25, 0.25, 0.25, 0.25)$. Given these parameters, the target values are not achieved for KPI1 and KPI2. Adaption allows to reach the target value for KPI2 already after the third cycle with $\mathbf{v} = (0.32, 0.16, 0.36, 0.16)$. The value of KPI1 changes from 0.65 to 0.75 though the target value cannot be achieved. The final set of weights is $(0.277, 0.102, 0.518, 0.103)$.

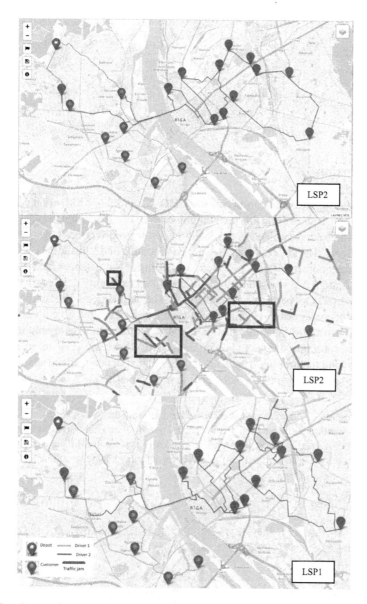

Fig. 3. Routing results for LSP2 (upper panel), LSP2 including traffic jams data (middle panel) and LSP2 (bottom panel). Notable differences are marked with green dots (lower panel) and traffic jams avoided by LSP1 are marker with blue boxes (middle panel). (Color figure online)

Table 2. KPI weights and values depending on the adaption cycle

Adaption cycle	KPI weights **v**	KPI1	KPI2	KPI3	KPI4
1	(0.25, 0.25, 0.25, 0.25)	0.65	0.92	1.25	1.22
2	(0.3, 0.2, 0.3, 0.2)	0.65	0.89	1.25	1.03
3	(0.32, 0.16, 0.36, 0.16)	0.65	1.18	1.25	1.20
4	(0.312, 0.128, 0.432, 0.128)	0.75	1.03	1.25	1.33
5	(0.277, 0.102, 0.518, 0.103)	0.75	1.01	1.25	1.61

6   Conclusion

The paper investigates applicability of the CDD methodology for solving the vehicle routing problem. It shows that this methodology can be used to design the vehicle routing capability, which serves as a basis of providing customized services to various logistics service providers. The key concepts used are KPI, context and adjustments. KPI describe vehicle routing objectives, context defines routing circumstances and adjustments encapsulate routing decision-making logics and adapt capability delivery depending on context situation and performance observed. The adjustments are implemented as context-dependent algorithms optimizing attainment of specified objectives.

The vehicle routing capability is design and adjustments for route optimization and adaptation of routing parameters are implemented. These are used in an illustrative example showing that routing results are indeed context dependent and adaption allows to improve routing performance by balancing multiple-criteria.

Acknowledgments. This research has received funding from the research project "Competence Centre of Information and Communication Technologies" of EU Structural funds, contract No. 1.2.1.1/16/A/007 signed between IT Competence Centre and Central Finance and Contracting Agency, Research No. 1.6 "Support for multi-criteria enterprise vehicle routing".

References

1. Armbrust, M., Fox, A., Griffith, R., Joseph, A.D., Katz, R., Konwinski, A., Lee, G., Patterson, D., Rabkin, A., Stoica, I., Zaharia, M.: A view of cloud computing. Commun. ACM 53(4), 50–58 (2010)
2. Chang, J.G., Sun, W., Huang, Y., Zhi, H.W., Gao, B.: A framework for native multi-tenancy application development and management. In: Proceedings - The 9th IEEE International Conference on E-Commerce Technology; The 4th IEEE International Conference on Enterprise Computing, E-Commerce and E-Services, CEC/EEE 2007, p. 551 (2007)
3. Bĕrziša, S., Bravos, G., González, T., Czubayko, U., España, S., Grabis, J., Henkel, M., Jokste, L., Kampars, J., Koç, H., Kuhr, J., Llorca, C., Loucopoulos, P., Pascual, R.J., Pastor, O., Sandkuhl, K., Simic, H., Stirna, J., Giromé, F.V., Zdravkovic, J.: Capability driven development: an approach to designing digital enterprises. Bus. Inform. Syst. Eng. 57, 15–25 (2015)
4. Zdravkovic, J., Pastor, Ó., Loucopoulos, P.: Selected topics on advances in capability-oriented information systems development: editorial introduction to issue 10 of CSIMQ. Complex Syst. Inf. Model. Q. CSIMQ 10, I–II (2017)

5. Braekers, K., Ramaekers, K., van Nieuwenhuyse, I.: The vehicle routing problem: state of the art classification and review. Comput. Ind. Eng. **99**, 300–313 (2016)

6. Eksioglu, B., Vural, A.V., Reisman, A.: The vehicle routing problem: a taxonomic review. Comput. Ind. Eng. **57**, 1472–1483 (2009)

7. Cardoso, Pedro J.S., Schütz, G., Semião, J., Monteiro, J., Rodrigues, J., Mazayev, A., Ey, E., Viegas, M.: Integration of a real-time stochastic routing optimization software with an enterprise resource planner. In: Grueau, C., Gustavo Rocha, J. (eds.) GISTAM 2015. CCIS, vol. 582, pp. 124–141. Springer, Cham (2016). doi:10.1007/978-3-319-29589-3_8

8. Giaglis, G.M., Minis, I., Tatarakis, A., Zeimpekis, V.: Minimizing logistics risk through real-time vehicle routing and mobile technologies. Int. J. Phys. Distrib. Logistics Manage. **34**(9), 749–764 (2004)

9. Grabis, J., Kampars, J.: Design of capability delivery adjustments. In: Krogstie, J., Mouratidis, H., Su, J. (eds.) CAiSE 2016. LNBIP, vol. 249, pp. 52–62. Springer, Cham (2016). doi: 10.1007/978-3-319-39564-7_5

10. Jozefowiez, N., Semet, F., Talbi, E.-G.: Multi-objective vehicle routing problems. Eur. J. Oper. Res. **189**(2), 293–309 (2008)

11. Kallehauge, B., Larsen, J., Madsen, O.B.G., Solomon, M.M.: Vehicle routing problem with time windows. In: Desaulniers, G., et al. (eds.) Column Generation, pp. 67–98. Springer, New York (2005)

Aligning Software Architecture and Business Strategy with Continuous Business Engineering

Kurt Sandkuhl[✉]

Institute of Computer Science, Rostock University, Albert-Einstein-Str. 22,
18057 Rostock, Germany
Kurt.Sandkuhl@uni-rostock.de

Abstract. Continuous Engineering (CE) investigates fundamentals and basic principles of evolution in IT-engineering processes. Continuous Software Engineering (CSE) applies these principles in the context of software engineering and develops methodologies, concepts and techniques for evolvable software systems. Continuous business engineering (CBE) is closely related to principles of CE and the research field of CSE. The main purpose of this position paper is to extend earlier work on CBE by integrating the concept of capabilities. The paper describes the scope of CBE research, investigates connections to other research fields and discusses approaches in the field of CBE for aligning software architecture, capabilities and business strategy.

Keywords: Continuous engineering · Continuous capability engineering · Business strategy

1 Introduction

Most enterprises and public authorities nowadays are highly dependant on their IT-infrastructure and IT-applications to preserve their competitiveness in a global market. In particular in industry domains and service sectors, where the whole value chain has to be supported by IT, it is crucial to have solutions which are flexible in case of changes in business model or market environment. Examples are the utility sector and the banking industry. In these application fields it is of economic and strategic importance to be able to quickly adapt software systems to changes in customers' requirements, business goals or company processes. Evolution of software systems in alignment to business strategy has become a core issue. This issue is even more emphasized, as most domain-specific infrastructures are long-living. They incorporate process and product knowledge of the individual owners and often were optimized over several decades. In financial industries, for example, there are still software components in use developed in the 1980s. These components cannot simply be redesigned and replaced by new components in state-of-the-art technology, as this would require big investments, bear high risks and questionable business benefits.

Furthermore, the topic of adaptability is not a new one but has been under discussion since many years. According to a study by the META-Group in 2000, senior business executives from US-based fortune 500 companies were not satisfied with the

A. Metzger and A. Persson (Eds.): CAiSE 2017 Workshops, LNBIP 286, pp. 14–26, 2017.
DOI: 10.1007/978-3-319-60048-2_2

contribution of the information technology (IT) in their enterprises: only 12% of all IT-projects contributed from their point of view significantly to reach strategic goals [5]. A survey of McKinsey from 2014 shows that priorities of enterprises shifted towards service innovation and digitization, but the pressure on IT regarding adaptiveness and contribution to business value still exists [11]. This confirms the need for aligning IT-infrastructure with the business strategy to increase the business value of information technology. This also underlines the high attention that most medium and large businesses pay to their internal IT. But what is the contribution of information technology to the success of the enterprise? What is its business value? Does the infrastructure support changes in the business strategy in an adequate way?

During the last twenty years, a number of research projects and activities have investigated the issue of "business value of information technology", including the fields of IT-controlling [9], evaluation of software architectures [6], or strategic management [7]. The field of Continuous Business Engineering (CBE) contributes to this research area by addressing the joint evolution of business capabilities and IT-infrastructure in an enterprise or organization. A capability is the ability and capacity that enable an enterprise to achieve a business goal in a given context [1]. Business goals are means for designing and expressing the business strategy of an enterprise.

CBE aims at integrating formulation and implementation processes on business strategy level and engineering processes on IT-infrastructure level. We consider this task as continuously ongoing process dedicated to ensure integrated evolution of business model and IT-infrastructure. CBE has to integrate various research aspects, like continuous transformation of business goals into capabilities, continuous transformation of capabilities into IT-infrastructures, continuous development of software and systems architectures, etc. CBE therefore investigates methods, concepts and technologies for linking together business oriented models and technical models.

Continuous business engineering is closely related to the principles of Continuous Engineering (CE) and the research field of Continuous Software Engineering (CSE). CE investigates fundamentals and basic principles of evolution in IT-engineering processes. CSE applies these principles in the context of software engineering and develops methodologies, concepts and techniques for evolvable software systems (see Sect. 2). In a simplified picture, CBE can be described as defining correspondences between a model of the business strategy and a model of the IT-infrastructure. Section 4 of this paper describes three approaches for linking these models based on different degrees of coupling: (a) describing the business strategy based on a balanced scorecard and linking the software architecture via indicators, (b) combining the balanced scorecard approach with enterprise ontologies, and (c) integration of business strategy and software architecture in a joint enterprise model.

The main purpose of this position paper is to extend earlier work in the field [18] by describing the scope of CBE research, identifying connections to other research fields and investigating approaches in the field of CBE for aligning software architecture and business strategy. These aspects are reflected in the structure of the following sections: Sect. 2 summarizes current activities in CE and CSE. Section 3 introduces the notion and scope of CBE, and related research subjects. Section 4 introduces approaches for aligning business strategy and software architecture.

2 Continuous Software Engineering

Continuous Engineering investigates fundamentals and core principles of evolution in IT-engineering processes. Continuous Software Engineering (CSE) [14] applies these principles in the field of software engineering by researching, developing and applying methodologies, concepts and techniques for evolvable software systems.

One of the core goals of CSE are long-living, evolvable software systems of high quality that can be forward developed continuously [8]. An essential part of CSE is to achieve consistency and transparency between (a) all artifacts of a software development process within a development cycle (e.g. requirements, specification, architecture design, and implementation) and (b) the various forward development cycles of a software system and their modifications. This requires the identification of variations, invariants and dependencies in order to predict the potential impact of initial and induced modifications. CSE is based on a series of integrated methods and concepts. The most important among them are:

Model-driven Development: CSE is based on a defined and highly mature engineering process defining all development activities with tasks and expected results. Results of all activities are represented as formalized models and transformation from activity to activity is defined.

Components as the Basis of Software Systems: Components encapsulate clearly defined functionality made available via interfaces. Components can be newly designed or refactored from a legacy system. CSE provides approaches how components together with their interfaces, invariants and contexts should be identified, modeled and described.

Reference Architectures for Application Areas: Software reference architecture defines the general structure of the applications of an application area. It also determines which components should be available, as well as required aids for the software developer, such as architectural templates for designing a system.

Support for the Software Development Process: CSE aims to integrate specification, design and documentation methods, as well as the use of reference architectures or architectural templates into the software construction process. In order to do so, special guidelines and aids for different processes are developed in the framework of continuous software engineering.

Evolution Strategies: A variety of reasons can be the cause for forward development or changes in software systems. These reasons include, for example, changes in business models, new requirements from regulators or modifications to the service or technical infrastructure. Reasons for and situations of change can be categorized and derived from evolution scenarios. CSE defines process models for these scenarios and procedures for designing software systems.

Management and Organizational Techniques: In addition to the continuous evolution of software systems and communication infrastructures, even the development and evolution processes require monitoring, control and continuous redesigned. Thus, their management and organizational techniques are observed in the context of CSE.

3 Continuous Business Engineering

3.1 Notion and Scope

Continuous business engineering can be defined as engineering process integrating forward-development and management processes on business level (i.e. for business strategy and capabilities required for implementing business strategies) and engineering processes on IT-infrastructure level. CBE investigates continuous transformation of business goals into capabilities, continuous development of IT-infrastructures in support of capabilities, continuous evaluation of IT-infrastructure with respect to business needs, continuous improvement of software and infrastructure engineering process, continuous development of software and systems architectures, etc. CBE therefore develops methods, concepts and technologies for linking together business oriented models and technical models.

In a simplified picture, continuous business engineering can be described as defined correspondence between business strategy and model of IT-infrastructure:

- On business strategy level, a model exits expressing the business strategy of the organisation in question. Capability models have proven to be suitable for this purpose [12]. Capabilities are the ability and capacity that enable an enterprise to achieve a business goal in a given context. Development and evolution of this model is performed and controlled by a management process.
- On IT-infrastructure level, a model exists representing the existing IT-infrastructure and/or the software architecture of the organization in question. Forward-development and evolution of this model is performed and controlled by an engineering process.

Between business strategy and model of IT-infrastructure correspondences exist. These correspondences enable control, assessment and supervision of the IT-infrastructure with respect to the business needs expressed in a business strategy. The link between business model and model of IT-infrastructure will cause a number of benefits for the enterprise and open various possibilities of triggering activities in the IT-infrastructure when changes in the business model occur. We expect advantages in

- Identifying work processes, organisational structures and software components faster that will be affected by changes in business strategy. This will lead to shorter innovation cycles in the IT-infrastructure,
- Identifying the potential for innovation in the business strategy and business model easily implementable due to existing capabilities,
- Assessing and evaluating the business value of the IT-infrastructure. If correspondences between business model and IT-model are defined, this implicitly will include criteria for evaluation of the infrastructure. Continuous assessment of IT-infrastructure will be possible.

3.2 Related Research Subjects

Besides the connection to CE, CBE is related to a number of research subjects contributing concepts, methods or technologies for linking business and engineering.

Knowledge Modelling: We see methods for describing semantics of IT-components and services as well as for describing intentions of business strategies and objectives as one of the key technologies for CBE. This includes approaches in the field of ontologies and topic maps as well as related standards and services. Relevant issues in this area are knowledge representation techniques, semantic match-making, competence modeling, evolution scenarios for information models with technologies like topic maps, semantic nets or semantic web technologies.

Capability Management: Recent progress in the area of capability management showed the importance of explicating the deployment context of business services, which implement capabilities, and to use the context for adjustments during business service delivery [2]. This way of abstracting from deployment contexts and adding flexibility and adaptability to operations is an important contribution to achieve CBE.

System-Integration and dis-Integration: one specific research subject connected to CBE is the area of system-integration and dis-integration. System integration issues arise whenever inter-enterprise solutions and software systems have to be implemented, e.g. in networks of suppliers, project-based joint venture between companies or electronic business scenarios. In the field of system-integration, CBE aims at providing mechanisms for dynamic integration between a set of IT-infrastructures. As interoperability on communication and service level is widely available due to standards, the focus should be on business model level. Dynamic integration on this level includes the detection of suitable capabilities and there implementation according to the business needs, selection of the best implementation and integration of the selected service into the infrastructure. For this task a service description only including specifications of the interface (syntax, semantics) and communication protocols is not sufficient (WSDL, .NET). We are aiming at using additional conceptual descriptions and match-making based on these description.

Relevant issues in this area are component model including semantic component description for IT-infrastructures, definition of invariants and interdependencies (constraints), reference architectures and architecture patterns for evolvable it infrastructure, evolution scenarios based on component model with technologies like systems management platforms, light-weight integration protocols.

IT-Assessment: The field of IT-assessment aims at evaluating the quality of IT-infrastructures with respect to the business strategy. Changes in business strategy cause evolution requirements for technical infrastructure. CBE aims at predicting where changes are necessary, define parameters for construction for longevity.

Relevant issues in this area are definition of target systems for IT strategy; mapping from business models to capabilities to IT infrastructures; evaluation of process, product, and organizational quality; competence modelling as basis for assessments; evolution scenarios for IT strategies and business models with technologies like balanced scorecard approaches, technical due diligence methods and benchmarking approaches.

4 Business Strategy, Capability and Software Alignment

Starting from the concepts of CSE, this section proposes three approaches for linking software architecture and business strategy: (a) describing the business strategy based on a balanced scorecard and linking capabilities and software architecture via indicators, (b) combining the balanced scorecard approach with enterprise ontologies, and (c) integration of business strategy, capability and software & service architecture in a joint enterprise model. These approaches are an extension of earlier work in this field [18]. As they approaches incorporate different degrees of coupling, we will start with discussing this aspect.

4.1 Degrees of Coupling

Today's enterprises have to be capable to handle changes in various dimensions, including a number of external factors like changes in their markets (e.g. new competitor), in framework conditions (e.g. modified laws enforcing product features), in customers' demands (e.g. new functionality), or in their delivery processes (e.g. new technology increasing productivity). Similar to the system-oriented technical meaning of evolution, we can consider the enterprises process' of "purposeful stepwise advancement due to changes of the environment" adapting to changing environmental conditions in order to survive" as evolution.

Joint evolution of business strategy and IT-infrastructure has to be driven by the business perspective and requires a coupling between business strategy and software architecture. This opens possibilities for various integration levels between both. One extreme would be to automatically cause the necessary changes in the IT-infrastructure whenever changes in the business strategy occur. The other extreme of course is to do no integration at all and use the correspondences only for evaluation and assessment purposes. Between these two poles, various levels of integration can be achieved depending on formalization level of both models.

In our investigations, we distinguish different degrees of coupling (loose vs. tight) characterised by possible actions to manage and control evolution:

- Supervision: monitoring performance or assessing compatibility to strategic objectives
- Initiate change process: definition of requirements and change requests and initiation of change processes, accordingly
- Configuration changes: change parameters or declarations for generic components or change configuration of overall system (no changes in the implementation)
- Architecture and design changes: introduce new software components or substitute existing components, e.g. based on architecture patterns or a component library
- System changes: modify design and implementation of the software system automatically.

4.2 Balanced Scorecard Approach

Contemporary management literature has discussed extensively the field of formation, description, and implementation of business strategies [13]. Although different approaches for modelling a business strategy exist, which are tailored to different sizes and natures of enterprises [16], the following elements are commonly seen as essential parts of a business strategy:

- Goals and targets to reach including time frames
- Actions dedicated to achieve goals and implement the targets
- Organizational units of the enterprise responsible for implementing the actions
- Indicators, policies, assessments and other means to evaluate the progress of implementing the business strategy
- Processes implementing measurement of indicator
- Management systems with roles and processes coordinating actions and forward development of the business strategy

It has been observed by a number of researchers that strategy formulation is a nontrivial task involving a number of strategic business units. Furthermore, strategy formulation and strategy implementation are difficult to integrate.

For our investigations, we will use the Balanced Scorecard approach from Kaplan and Norton [10] to capture and model business strategy. Although this approach does not provide an own modelling language, it has from our perspective a number of advantages, e.g. being adaptable to specific organizations and having achieved a broad usage within industry and public authorities, much research work and experience published, IT tools available to support modelling a scorecard and making it operational, and own experience in using this approach for modelling IT-Strategy [17].

The Balanced Scorecard approach was developed in order to complement the traditional financial accounting model, which is very much focused on past performance, with measures for drivers of organizational future performance. Thus, the Balanced Scorecard is seen as a means to establish the *balance* between financial and non-financial aspects when developing and implementing vision and strategy of the company. A typical balanced scorecard captures the business strategy of an enterprise in four perspectives:

- Financial perspective: which goals have to be reached to succeed financially?
- Customer perspective: what should be the image of the enterprise from a customer's perspective?
- Internal business perspective: what business processes must be excelled at?
- Learning and growth: how to sustain the ability to change and improve?

For each of these four perspectives, strategic objectives have to be defined clarifying the vision, and measurements have to be developed and linked to the objectives. The measurements typically are implemented based on performance indicators and processes for obtaining these indicators. In the context of complex organisations, Kaplan & Norton recommend to develop not only one corporate scorecard, but also a separate scorecard for each strategic business unit conducting activities in an entire value chain.

The balanced scorecard can be used as strategic management system, i.e. to develop the strategy over the long run. This requires implementation of a management cycle including setting targets and planning strategic initiatives how to reach them, establishing strategic feedback and learning, and reviewing business strategy and modifying the vision and objectives accordingly.

Our approach for linking the business strategy – explicated in a balanced scorecard – and the software architecture is to operationalize the actions required to achieve the business strategy in capabilities, which are made explicit in a capability model. Furthermore, the approach includes to develop a separate scorecard for the business unit responsible for software and service management and to integrate this software scorecard closely with the corporate scorecard. Close integration means that the software scorecard has to have the same perspectives as the corporate scorecard and that each objective of the software scorecard has to contribute to reach at least one objective of the corporate scorecard.

Measurements and performance indicators of the software scorecard can then be used for assessing and evaluating the software architectures contribution to implement the business strategy. This balanced scorecard approach has been applied successfully in a number of enterprises [17]. Capability models form an important contribution to this approach as they also explicate deployment contexts and dependencies between IT-based business service and the (software) services implementing them. Figure 1 visualizes the overall approach:

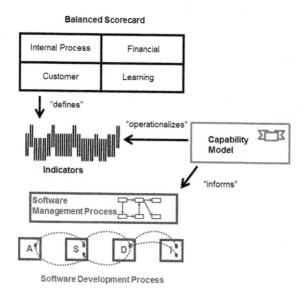

Fig. 1. Balanced Scorecard-based Approach to Alignment

4.3　Combing Enterprise Ontology and Balanced Scorecard

Linking business strategy and software architecture via a balanced scorecard provides only basic possibilities for aligned evolution. The indicators can be used to discover a tendency whether the IT-infrastructure supports the business strategy adequately; the capability models add how well different deployment contexts are supported. This is primarily a view on the past performance with only limited possibility to create a future projection. Aligning strategy and IT from our point of view also should include to predict the impact of a change in business strategy, e.g. to identify the software components involved and cause-effect-relationships between strategic targets and software architecture parts.

Our approach is to use concept paths in enterprise ontologies as meta-data for linking strategy, capability and software architecture (see Fig. 2). Enterprise ontologies [20] capture the concepts and terms of an enterprise or a strategic business unit and their relationships. In our approach, we cover three different perspectives of an enterprise in the ontology:

- work processes and tasks within the enterprise
- organizational structure in the enterprise including established roles
- product or service structure of an enterprise related to the business area

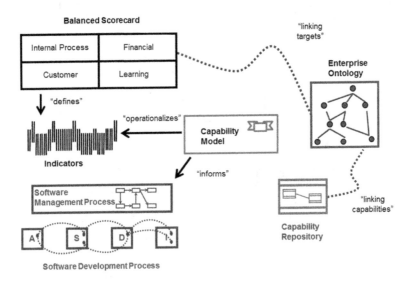

Fig. 2. BSC and EO Approach to Alignment

These perspectives can be represented by using semantic nets [15] or semantic technologies. The enterprise ontology provides possibility to define a mapping between capability, software component and business strategy via concept paths: For each capability required for implementing a business strategy and every software component being part of the architecture, the work processes, roles, and organization structures supported by this capability and component are identified by defining concept paths in the ontology. A concept path is a sequence of concepts being connected by associations in the ontology [3].

At the same time, roles, processes and services/products with high importance for strategic objectives are identified and linked to these objectives via concept paths. Thus, an intentional model and more formalized representation corresponding to the business strategy is created. Linking of business strategy and software architecture, e.g. in order to identify which components will be affected in case of strategy changes, requires a mapping between concept paths representing the strategic objectives and concepts paths representing the software components. This matching based on concept paths already has been applied in a number of projects in the context of Web-Portals [4].

4.4 Enterprise Knowledge Modeling

The combination of Balanced Scorecard and Enterprise Ontology extends the possibilities for alignment from indicator-based performance evaluation to further formalization of business strategy and contributes to prediction of impact of changes. But it does not allow to automatically initiate and perform changes in components or a systems configuration of system. This goal requires from our point of view a tighter coupling with sound formalization, e.g. by integration of both, business strategy, capability and software architecture, within a joint model. This model, represented in a suitable modeling language, either must provide possibility to express elements and relationships for both areas or it has to integrate existing modeling approaches, e.g. Balanced Scorecard and CSE, in a single meta-model.

Numerous enterprise modeling approaches have been developed that integrate business and IT-viewpoints in a single model. Examples are Zachman's framework, TOGAF or the GERAM activities (see [19] for an overview to approaches). The Zachman framework for enterprise architecture structures representation of enterprise and system knowledge in two dimensions. The first dimension includes various viewpoints: data, function, network, people, time and motivation. The second dimension consists of abstraction levels: scope, business model, system model, technology model, detailed representations and functioning enterprise. From a theoretical point of view, i.e. looking at the completeness of the modeling approach, these concepts have the potential to implement the required tight coupling and support joint evolution. Furthermore, work con capability management and capability design and delivery (CDD) contributed an approach which supports co-evolution of business strategy and IT-based business services [2].

Based on our experience from earlier alignment projects, we see at least two aspects to be investigated in future research: Business strategy includes a lot more than processes, objectives and indicators. A holistic approach would have to take into account business culture, innovation processes, or organizational competences, which are to a large extent creative and hard to capture in a technical model. These aspects clearly would have to be simplified or excluded, when developing an enterprise model based on the above-mentioned approaches, the effect being a loss of context information and semantics, and of cause-effect-relationships. Medium-sized and even large enterprises have problems to provide a fairly complete software architecture model or a well-defined business strategy. Development of an enterprise model integrating both aspects will be in many cases not feasible due to missing information.

4.5 Conclusion

Based on the component-based and model-driven concepts from CSE for modeling the software architecture, we have presented three approaches to define correspondences providing different levels of support for joint evolution. Using our classification from Sect. 4.1, we can put these approaches into relationship with respect to their degree of coupling:

The balanced scorecard approach only facilitates a loose coupling between business strategy and software architecture based on indicators. This coupling supports supervision of the software architecture but no stronger integration. Balanced scorecard in combination with enterprise ontology enables us to identify software components that are affected by changes. Based on this, initiation of changes is possible, being a higher degree of coupling. Enterprise modelling supports the highest degree of coupling by promising – at least from a model point of view – to initiate and perform system changes in case of changes in the business strategy.

5 Summary

The business models of many enterprises nowadays are highly dependent on their IT-infrastructure. In order to preserve the competitiveness in a global market, it is crucial for them from a business perspective to quickly implement new business services, to react to new market demands or to implement new regulations. In this context, it is of decisive economic and strategic importance from a technical perspective to be able to quickly adapt software systems to changes. Alignment of IT-infrastructure with business strategy has become a core issue. The approach of Continuous Business Engineering (CBE) contributes to this challenge by addressing the joint evolution of business strategy, capabilities and software architecture. CBE aims at integrating forward-development on business strategy level and engineering processes on capability and software architecture level. We consider this task as a continuously ongoing process dedicated to ensure integrated evolution. In a simplified picture, CBE can be described as defining correspondences between a model of the business strategy and a model of capabilities and the software architecture.

This paper describes the scope of CBE research, identifies connections to other research fields and to investigates three approaches in the field of CBE based on different degrees of coupling: (a) describing the business strategy based on a balanced scorecard and linking the architecture model via indicators, (b) combining the balanced scorecard approach with enterprise ontologies, and (c) integration of business strategy, capabilities and software architecture in a joint enterprise model. Future work in the context of these approaches will be dedicated to (a) elaborating the advantages and limitations of the three different approaches, (b) a more detailed comparison to enterprise architecture management and capability management, and (c) applications in real-world projects in order to verify the potential.

References

1. Ahlemann, F., Stettiner, E., Messerschmidt, M., Legner, C.: Strategic Enterprise Architecture Management: Challenges, Best Practices, and Future Developments, p. 2012. Springer, Berlin (2012)
2. Bērziša, S., et al.: Capability driven development: approach to designing digital enterprises. Bus. Inform. Syst. Eng. **57**(1), 15–25 (2015)
3. Billig, A., Sandkuhl, K., Wendt, A.: Basic support for evolutionary web-portals: the BaSeWeP approach. In: Proceedings of the IASTED 2000, Las Vegas, November 2000
4. Billig, A., Sandkuhl, K.: Match-Making based on semantic nets: the XML-based BaSeWeP approach. In: Proceedings XSW 2002. Springer (2002)
5. Buchanan, D., Soley, R.: Aligning Enterprise Architecture and IT-Investments with Corporate Goals. META-Group (2002). http://www.metagroup.com/
6. Clements, P., Kazman, R., Klein, M.: Evaluating Software Architectures. Addison-Wesley Professional, October 2001
7. Croteau, A.-M., Bergeron, F.: An information technology trilogy: business strategy, technological deployment and organizational performance. J. Strateg. Inform. Syst. **10**, 77–99 (2001). Elsevier
8. Grosse-Rhode, M., Kutsche, R., Bübl, F.: Concepts for the Evolution of Component-Based Software Systems. Technical report, Fraunhofer ISST, Germany, October 2000
9. Hochstrasser, B., Griffiths, C.: Controlling IT Investment: Strategy and Management. International Thomson Business Press (1991)
10. Kaplan, R., Norton, D.: Balanced Scorecard. Harvard Business School Press, Boston (1996)
11. Khan, N., Sikes, J.: IT under pressure: McKinsey Global Survey results. McKinsey, March 2014. http://www.mckinsey.com/business-functions/digital-mckinsey/our-insights/it-under-pressure-mckinsey-global-survey-results
12. Koç, H., Kuhr, J.-C., Sandkuhl, K., Timm, F.: Capability-driven development - a novel approach to design enterprise capabilities. In: El-Sheikh, E., Zimmermann, A., Jain, L.C. (eds.) Emerging Trends in the Evolution of Service-Oriented and Enterprise Architectures. ISRL, vol. 111, pp. 151–177. Springer, Cham (2016). doi:10.1007/978-3-319-40564-3_9
13. Littler, K., Aisthorpe, P., Hudson, R., Keasey, K.: A new approach to linking strategy formulation and strategy implementation. Int. J. Inform. Manage. **20**(6), 411–428. Elsevier Science, December 2000
14. Müller, H., Weber, H. (eds.): Continuous Engineering of Industrial Scale Software Systems. Dagstuhl Seminar #98092, Report No. 203, Schloss Dagstuhl, March 1998
15. Nilsson, N.: Principles of Artificial Intelligence. Springer, Heidelberg (1982)
16. Quezada, L., et al.: A methodology for formulating a business strategy in manufacturing firms. Int. J. Prod. Econ. **60–61**, 87–94 (1999). Elsevier
17. Sandkuhl, K., Gohlke-Micknis, S., Hacker, J., Jakoby, A.: Die IT-StrategieCard - Ein Zielsystem für strategische IT-Themen auf Basis der Balanced Scorecard. Proc. Wirtschaftsinformatik 2001, Augsburg, September 2001
18. Sandkuhl, K., Smirnov, A.: Continuous business engineering: towards aligned evolution of business strategy and software architecture. In: Proceedings of the 10th ISPE International Conference on Concurrent Engineering, Madeira, Portugal (2003). ISBN 90 5809 622 X

19. Sandkuhl, K., Stirna, J., Persson, A., Wißotzki, M.: Enterprise Modeling: Tackling Business Challenges with the 4EM Method. The Enterprise Engineering Series. Springer, Heidelberg (2014). ISBN 978-3662437247
20. Uschold, M., et al.: The Enterprise Ontology. Artificial Intelligence Application Institute, Edinburgh (1997)

A Comparative Analysis of Concepts for Capability Design Used in Capability Driven Development and the NATO Architecture Framework

Janis Stirna[(✉)]

Department of Computer and Systems Sciences,
Stockholm University, Postbox 7003, 164 07 Kista, Sweden
js@dsv.su.se

Abstract. Recently an approach for information system design and delivery according to run-time context has been developed. It uses the concept of capability to express the organization's ability and capacity that enables it to achieve a business goal in a certain context, and hence is denoted Capability Driven Development (CDD). The concept of capability has also been used in other approaches because it facilitates business investment focus, it can be used as a baseline for business planning, and it directly leads to service specification and design. For example, several Enterprise Architecture frameworks have included capability as a key concept for analyzing organization's abilities to deliver desired functions. A notable contribution in this area is The NATO Architecture Framework (NAF), which aims at being a de facto standard for organizations operating in the areas of NATO. This paper analyses the possibilities of mapping the CDD concepts to NAF concepts that are relevant for capability design.

Keywords: Capability · Enterprise architecture · Enterprise modeling

1 Introduction

Linguistically, capability means *the ability or qualities necessary to do something* [1]. The notion of capability has been discussed throughout the past decades in application areas such as competence-based management, enterprise architecture management, developing firm's competitive advantage [2, 3], and, lately, Business-IT alignment [4]. Following the principles for specifying the organization's capacity and abilities to perform a business function, an approach called Capability Driven Development (CDD) has been developed [5].

CDD addresses the need for today's information system (IS) development frameworks and methodologies to support organizations acting in highly competitive and volatile environments, e.g. dealing with unexpected events, such as unpredicted increase of customer demands, legislation changes, new customer types, new alliances and competitors. The current business trends require companies to be able to operate continuously in dynamically changing business conditions [6, 7].

© Springer International Publishing AG 2017
A. Metzger and A. Persson (Eds.): CAiSE 2017 Workshops, LNBIP 286, pp. 27–38, 2017.
DOI: 10.1007/978-3-319-60048-2_3

The CDD methodology is based on Enterprise Modeling (EM), context modeling, variability modeling, adjustment algorithms, and patterns for capturing best practices. It is also supported by the CDD environment that allows capability design and runtime monitoring and adjustment.

Capability is used in a wide variety of approaches and frameworks and while there are clearly identifiable similarities, there are also substantial differences in its use. If CDD is to succeed in being adopted by a broader community it needs to address standardization in the respective area of development. There are four basic options to consider, namely,

(1) to propose a new standard,
(2) to influence an existing standard, i.e. to make it change or to incorporate a new proposal,
(3) to align with an existing standard or standards, or
(4) do nothing related to standards, in the hope that the industry take-up will be fast and widespread enough to establish a de-facto standard in a "grass-roots" way.

Options 1 and 2 are unrealistic to carry out without significant and probably world-wide backing of key industrial players, especially in areas where existing standards are already developed. We consider the areas of IS development and Enterprise Architecture (EA) which are the primary targets of the CDD methodology being such. Hence, applying Option 3 of analyzing the existing landscape of standards and proposing alignments of CDD with the more prominent contributions in the field is the most appropriate path to choose. For a product such as the CDD methodology and environment, Option 4 is too risky because there are a significant number of standards existing in this area.

To this end, the objective of the paper is *to analyze how capability is addressed by one prominent EA framework, namely, The NATO Architecture Framework (NAF)*. The aim of this analysis is to show how CDD modeling components correspond to those of NAF in order to support application scenarios such as analyzing enterprise architectures documented according to NAF and then operationalizing them with CDD in order to monitor and adjust the runtime execution.

The remainder of the paper is organized as follows. Section 2 briefly presents the approaches and frameworks that use the concept of capability, including more details of CDD and NAF. The analysis of CDD and NAF concepts is provided in Sect. 3. Concluding remarks are presented in Sect. 4.

2   Background to Approaches Using Capability

The notion of capability has a growing presence in the current business and IT alignment and development frameworks. It is used by business-oriented frameworks, such as Business Architecture and Business Modeling as well as in the alignment-oriented frameworks for Enterprise Architecture (EA) and Enterprise Modeling (EM). The inclusion of the capability notion in the current development frameworks seems to have the following intensions: (a) for business planning, it is becoming recognized as a key component for describing strategies of what a core business does in order to deliver value; (b) for IS development, it makes IS designs more understandable to business stakeholders by enabling them to use the capability notion to describe their requirements; and (c) for IS run-time and maintenance, it supports configurability of operations on a higher level of abstraction than services, process, and components.

The following areas of development approaches using the concept of capability can be identified:

- OMG Business Architecture (BA) [8]. It is an enterprise blueprint aiming to provide a common understanding of an organization, as well as to align strategic objectives with tactical demands.
- OMG Value Delivery Modeling Language (VDML) [9]. It defines a modeling language for analysis and design of the operations of an enterprise with a focus on the creation and exchange of value.
- The Open Group Architecture Framework (TOGAF) [10] describes architecture domains, concepts and methods for designing, using, and maintaining an enterprise architecture.
- ArchiMate is an EA modeling language [11]. It provides an architectural approach to describe and visualize different concepts of the types: active structure, behavior, and objects, as well as it defines their relations.
- The Department of Defense Architecture Framework (DODAF) [12] is an architecture framework for the US Department of Defense that provides visualization infrastructure for specific stakeholders concerns organized by various viewpoints.
- The UKMinistry of Defence Architecture Framework (MODAF) [13] is an architecture framework that defines a standardized way of conducting EA originally developed by the UK Ministry of Defence.
- The NATO Architecture Framework (NAF) [14] is an EA framework developed by NATO. It will be described in more detail in Sect. 2.2. It has many commonalities with DODAF and MODAF. A key difference is that MODAF is a description framework, i.e. it does not have its own methodology, while the latest version of NAF has a methodology based on TOGAF. Considering at least the nominal intention of NAF being used by the large number of the NATO countries we have chosen NAF for the purpose of this analysis.
- OASIS SOA provides an abstract, foundation reference architecture addressing the ecosystem viewpoint for building and interacting within the SOA paradigm [15].
- The Open Group SOA Reference Architecture defines a consumer and provider perspective with cross-cutting concerns describing architecture building blocks and principles that support the realizations of SOA [16].
- SOA Modeling Language (SoaML) by OMG defining a small set of extensions to UML to support SOA modeling [17]; it can be seen as an instantiation of a subset of The Open Group's architecture for representing SOA artifacts in UML.

A more detailed analysis of how the above frameworks address capability in terms of modeling perspective, definition, purpose, and methodology is available in [18].

2.1   Capability Driven Development Methodology

The CDD methodology consists of method components [5]. To structure the methodology, the components have been divided into upper-level method components and method extensions. Each upper-level component describes a certain application area and may also contain sub-components. The upper-level method components are currently the following:

- *Capability Design Process* guiding how to design, evaluate, and develop capabilities by using process models, goal models, and other types of models.
- *Enterprise Modeling guiding* the creation of enterprise models that are used as input for capability design.
- *Context Modeling* analyzing the capability context and its variations needed to deal with business process variations.
- *Reuse of capability design* guiding the elicitation and documentation of patterns for capability design.
- *Run-time Delivery Adjustment* adjusting capability at runtime.

The overall CDD process includes three cycles (1) capability design; (2) capability delivery; and (3) capability refinement/updating. The capability design cycle often starts with *Enterprise Modeling*, i.e. by a business request for a new capability - the request might be initiated by strategic business planning, changes in context, or discovery of new business opportunities requiring reconfiguration of existing or the creation of new goals, business processes or services, and other EM elements. This is followed with a formalized definition of requested capabilities and definition of the relevant contexts according, linking with relevant capability delivery patterns, as well as supporting IT applications all of which as can be seen as part of *capability design*.

In addition, several method extensions addressing specific business challenges to which the CDD methodology have been developed.

CDD defines capability as *"the ability and capacity that enable an enterprise to achieve a business goal in a certain context."* The theoretical and methodological foundations for CDD is provided by the core capability meta-model (CMM) in Fig. 1, and in details presented in [5]. The CMM is developed on the basis of requirements from the industrial project partners, and related research on capabilities. In brief, the meta-model has three main sections:

- (a) *Enterprise model,* representing organizational designs with Goals, KPIs, Processes (with concretizations as Process Variants), and Resources. Key aspects are capability and goal dependency as well as capability and business process dependency showing intentional and operational aspects of each capability.
- (b) *Context,* represented with Context Set for which a Capability is designed and Context Situation at runtime that is monitored and according to which the deployed solutions should be adjusted. Context Indicators are used for measuring the context properties (Measuring Property); and
- (c) *Patterns,* for delivering Capability by reusable solutions for reaching Goals under different Context Situations. Each pattern describes how a certain Capability is to be delivered within a certain Context Situation and what Processes Variants and Resources are needed to support a Context Set.

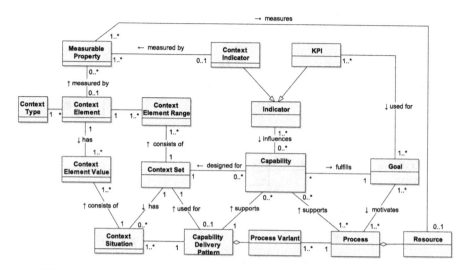

Fig. 1. A core meta-model for supporting Capability Driven Development [19].

Figure 1 is a simplified version of the CMM showing only the key components of CDD and omitting, for instance, constructs for representing goal decomposition relationships and process variants. The complete version including definitions of the components is available in [5, 19].

2.2   The NATO Architecture Framework

NAF is organized into a number of views such, All Views, Capability View, Operational View, System View, Service View, Technical View, and Programme View. Capability view, further specified in models addressing detailed aspects of capability development, namely: Capability taxonomy (C1), Enterprise Vision (C2), Capability dependencies (C3), Standard Processes (C4), Effects (C5), Performance Parameters (C7), Planning Assumptions (C8), and Capability Roadmap (Cr).

NAF defines capability as *"the ability of one or more resources to deliver a specified type of effect or a specified course of action"* [14]. Examples of capabilities according to NAF are "Tank production, 20 tanks per year", "Tank production, 20–40 tanks per year", "Light Armor Vehicle Recovery", and "Heavy Armor Vehicle Recovery". Details of the capability definition and associations is given in the NAF meta-model [14], see Figs. 2 and 3. The key associations of capability are as follows:

- Capabilities may be specialized into more specific capabilities, composed of several capabilities, as well as dependent on other capabilities.
- Capability when applied is associated with measurable categories
- Capability elaborated into Capability configuration package, which is used to configure resources for capability implementation.

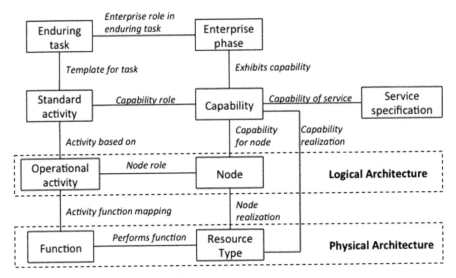

Fig. 2. A simplified overview of the NAF meta-model, adapted from [14].

– Enterprise phase exhibits a capability. The connection between capabilities and goals is realized through enduring phase of the enterprise.
– Capability supports an enduring task by defining capability for the task.

A more detailed meta-model of the Enterprise Vision view (C2) is shown in Fig. 3 on the basis of which the analysis of CDD and NAF was performed. The purpose of a C2 view is to provide a strategic context for the capabilities described in the architecture and to specify the scope for the architecture in terms of vision, goals, enduring tasks and capabilities.

NAF is interoperable with MODAF because it is based on earlier versions of MODAF. The interactive website of the NAF meta-model also has the ability to present NAF according to MODAF views. Hence this analysis is relevant even to those countries that are not part of NATO and use, as in the case of Swedish Armed Forces, MODAF instead.

3   Analysis of CDD and NAF Concepts

NAF addresses capability in the Capability Viewpoints (C1-C8). This section will analyze the key concepts of these viewpoints as defined in the NAF meta-model (see Figs. 2 and 3) with respect to the CDD meta-model (Fig. 1).

We will analyze the concepts of the NAF meta-model that are relevant to the five key areas addressed by CDD method components, namely, Capability Design (including Enterprise Modeling), Context Modeling, Business Process and Variability Modeling, Reuse and Patterns, as well as Adjustment Algorithms. These are mostly documented in NAF viewpoints C1 to C8 and Cr. Components form these viewpoints have been analyzed only if they have direct influence on the concept of capability, i.e. NAF

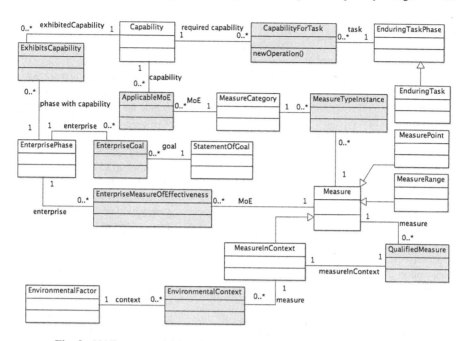

Fig. 3. NAF meta-model for view C2 Enterprise Vision, adapted from [14].

viewpoints addressing, for instance, services and other aspects of the architecture have been excluded from this paper.

Figure 3 shows a part of the meta-model of view C2 Enterprise Vision that have relations with capability and addresses similar components to the CMM. It uses the UML Class diagram notation; classes in color denote objectified relationships.

Table 1 shows the proposal for alignment of NAF concepts and CDD concepts. Considering the high complexity of the NAF meta-model we also indicate in which view of the meta-model the concept is chiefly used. The CDD meta-model is not structured in views although each of its method components focuses on a specific part of modeling and hence can be considered as dynamic views.

Table 1 shows constructs of both approaches that have similar purposes and are in principle interchangeable in the sense that they serve similar purposes. In several cases of mapping the NAF concepts to CDD the mapping would depend on the intensions of the modeling. E.g. in the case of Enduring task, since it is defined as "a specification of what the enterprise does", it would be our primary choice of modeling it with a CDD business process on a high level of decomposition. This would support clear visibility of how the process and process variants are used to deliver a capability. Another option, however, would be to model it with an operational goal, which would make the CDD model more understandable from a strategic perspective.

The constructs of NAF cover three of the key aspects of CDD, namely, Capability Design (including Enterprise Modeling), Context Modeling, and Business Process and Variability Modeling. The forth aspect of Reuse and Patterns is not explicitly addressed by NAF, but it can be covered by developing service specifications (NAF viewpoints

Table 1. A proposal for alignment of NAF and CDD concepts

NAF Concept	NAF view-point	Relevant CDD concept	Comments
Capability	C1	*Capability*	The main difference is that NAF definition of capability does not include the context dependence
Capability specialization relationship	C1	Capability *composition relationship*	NAF uses specialization to specify more generic capabilities into more specific capabilities. According to CDD all capabilities should be operational (not abstract) hence, composition of capability into more atomic sub-capabilities is more appropriate
Capability composition relationship	C3	Capability *composition relationship*	Both NAF and CDD have a relationship for specifying that one capability can be a part of another
Capability dependency relationship	C3	*Capability collaboration*	In NAF capability dependency relationship is used for analyzing the dependencies between capabilities and between capability clusters. CDD has a method extension for modeling capability collaboration, for a similar purpose
Measure Category	C1, C2	*Context Indicator KPI*	Measure Category is used for specifying Measures of Effectiveness relevant to Capabilities. CDD monitors capability by KPIs and Context Indicators both of which are based on Measurable properties
Capability relationship related to Measure Category	C2, C7	Capability relationship *influences Indicator*	According to NAF Capabilities are measured according to Measure Categories which are specified as Measures of Effectiveness (MoE) and are manifested by Measures when executed. This is similar to CDD measurement according to Indicators, which can be of two kinds – Context Indicator and KPI

(continued)

Table 1. (*continued*)

NAF Concept	NAF view-point	Relevant CDD concept	Comments
Statement of goal	C2	*Goal*	NAF and CDD goals are similar in their definition and relationships for goal dependencies and refinement
Goal has sub-goal relationship	C2	Goal refinement relationships *(motivates, hinders, AND, OR)*	CDD is based on 4EM and hence has a richer set of relationships for goal modeling. This can be explained by the fact that NAF is not intended for extensive goal modeling
Vision statement	C2	*Goal*	NAF's Vision Statement is a short paragraph outlining the vision for a given phase of an enterprise; it is a part of Enterprise Phase. In CDD terms, this is modeled by goals and the elaboration of a goal hierarchy
Enterprise Phase	C2		In NAF Enterprise Phase denotes an UndertakingState that is a current or future state of a WholeLifeEnterprise, e.g. as-is or to-be. CDD does not have a specific construct for modeling phases of organization transformation. This is usually achieved by structuring the model into views and sub-models
Measure	C2	*Measureable property, Context Element*	In NAF Measure can be specialized into Measure In Context which in turn can be linked to Environmental Factor, and into Measure Range. These concepts are similar to the ones provided by the Context Modeling method component of CDD, specifically Measureable Property, Context Element, and Context Element Range
Measure in Context	C2	*Context Element, Measurable Property*	NAF has Measure In Context as a measure in a specific Environmental Factor such as Terrain Type, Weather etc. This can be modeled with the CDD

(*continued*)

Table 1. (*continued*)

NAF Concept	NAF view-point	Relevant CDD concept	Comments
			concepts Context Element and Measurable Property
Capability relation to Enterprise Phase	C2		In CDD, phases of the change management process are realized by model structure, hence such relationship is not present on a conceptual level
Enduring task	C2	*Process*	In NAF Enduring task is seen as an undertaking recognized by an enterprise as being essential to achieving its goals - i.e. a strategic specification of what the enterprise does. This concept is similar to CDD business Process at a higher level of decomposition. I.e. capability is delivered by a business process, but the actual context variations are achieved by process variants
Capability relation to Enduring Task	C2	Capability *requires* *Process*	In NAF Enduring task is a sub-class of Enduring Task Phase, and the purpose of the relationship is to specify what Capability is required in order for an Enterprise to conduct a phase of an Enduring Task. In CDD this is realized by the relationship Capability requires Process
Standard Activity	C4	*Process*	NAF defined Standard Activity as a ProcessType that is a standard procedure (e.g. doctrinal tasks). Standard activity can consist of other Standard Activities and is based on Operational Activity. This is modeled as Process in CDD
Capability relationship has role in Standard Activity	C4	Capability *requires* *Process*	In NAF this relationship is used to specify that a Capability participate in a StandardActivity. In CDD the same can be achieved by tracing all relationships between Capability and Processes and Process Variants

S1 to S8). The fifth aspect of CDD, namely, Adjustment Algorithms, is not explicitly addressed by NAF and hence additional workarounds might need to be used for instance in the Logical viewpoints.

Concerning the way of working, CDD offers well elaborated method guidance and extensive supporting material. In contrast, currently the method guidance for NAF is based on the Architecture Development Method (ADM) of TOGAF, but it is still a work in progress.

In terms of tool support CDD offers an integrated environment for capability design and runtime monitoring and adjustment while the tools that support NAF primarily focus on architecture design and documentation. The current status of the CDD environment allows adjustment and configuration of existing systems, such as ERP systems. To support cases when a new IS needs to be developed to realize capability delivery, an ongoing work on supporting capability designs with Model Driven Development is reported in [20].

4 Concluding Remarks

In this paper we have summarized how the concept of capability is used in CDD and NAF for the purpose of aligning CDD with an established EA framework. While there are differences in capability definitions, meta-models, and the way it should be modeled, both use capability to bind the intentional part of the organizational design with the operational part that also encompasses variability/alternatives.

We can conclude that NAF has a more generic scope; hence it includes more constructs for strategic planning and specification of IT architecture. CDD mostly focuses on operational capability design and execution of the adjustments. Hence CDD is more streamlined when it comes to modeling enterprise designs in terms of goals, processes, resources, and best practices (patterns). CDD also supports monitoring capability performance in terms of context elements and KPI as well as specification of adjustment algorithms that are automatically deployed in the Capability Navigation Application. While NAF defines measures of effectiveness, development of monitoring and adjustment applications can be seen as aspects of Model Driven Development, which beyond the main purpose of NAF and hence it does not explicitly support them.

The overall approach taken in the project that developed the CDD methodology has been to focus on the elaboration of proposals for CDD alignment with significant standards that are used in practice which in turn support broader adoption of CDD. The analysis performed in this paper supports the application scenario of elaborating capability designs with CDD from existing organizational designs expressed according to NAF. Such a way of working would contribute to implementing the aspects of runtime monitoring and adjustment of information systems according to context changes for which NAF currently does not offer explicit support.

References

1. Oxforddictionaries.com. Capability, Oxford Advanced Learner's Dictionary. http://www.oxforddictionaries.com/definition/learner/capability
2. Collis, J.D.: How valuable are organizational capabilities? Strateg. Manag. J. **15**, 143–152 (1994). Wiley
3. Teece, D.J., Pisano, G., Shuen, A.: Dynamic capabilities and strategic management. Strateg. Manag. J. **18**(7), 509–533 (1997)
4. Bhatt, G.D., Grover, V.: Types of information technology capabilities and their role in competitive advantage: an empirical study. J. Manag. Inf. Syst. **22**(2), 253–277 (2005)
5. Grabis, J., Henkel, M., Kampars, J., Koç, H., Sandkuhl, K., Stamer, D., Stirna, J., Valverde, F., Zdravkovic, J.: D5.3 The final version of Capability driven development methodology, FP7 proj. 611351 CaaS – Capability as a Service in digital enterprises, doi:10.13140/RG.2.2.35862.34889
6. Lucke, C., Krell, S., Lechner, U.: Critical issues in enterprise architecting - a literature review. In: AMCIS 2010 (2010). http://aisel.aisnet.org/amcis2010/305
7. Stirna, J., Zdravkovic, J.: Interview with Sladjan Maras on challenges and needs in enterprise modeling. BISE J. **57**(1), 79–81 (2015)
8. OMG Business Architecture Special Interest Group&Guild. "What Is Business Architecture?" http://bawg.omg.org/, http://www.businessarchitectureguild.org/
9. OMG: Value Delivery Metamodel, v. 1.0 (2013). http://www.omg.org/spec/VDML/1.0/
10. The Open Group, TOGAF 9.1, a Standard. The Open Group. http://pubs.opengroup.org/architecture/togaf9-doc/arch/index.html
11. The Open Group. ArchiMate 2.1 Specification. The Open Group, December 2013. http://www.opengroup.org/archimate/downloads.htm
12. Department of Defense DoD Architecture Framework Version 2.0, 28 May 2009. http://dodcio.defense.gov/Portals/0/Documents/DODAF/DoDAF_v2-02_web.pdf
13. UK Ministry of Defence, MOD Architecture Framework (2012). https://www.gov.uk/guidance/mod-architecture-framework
14. UK Ministry of Defence, NATO Architecture Framework v4.0 Documentation (2013). http://nafdocs.org/modem
15. OASIS. SOA Reference Architecture 1.0. http://docs.oasis-open.org/soa-rm/soa-ra/v1.0/cs01/soa-ra-v1.0-cs01.pdf. Accessed 02 Mar 2016
16. The Open Group. SOA Reference Architecture, November 2011. https://www2.opengroup.org/ogsys/jsp/publications/PublicationDetails.jsp?publicationid=12490
17. OMG. Service oriented architecture Modeling Language (SoaML®), Version 1.0.1, May 2012. http://www.omg.org/spec/SoaML/1.0.1/
18. Zdravkovic, J., Stirna, J., Grabis, J.: A comparative analysis of using the capability notion for congruent business-and information systems engineering. Complex Syst. Inf. Model. Q., CSIMQ, 10, 1–20 (2017)
19. Bērziša, S., Bravos, G., Gonzalez Cardona, T., Czubayko, U., España, S., Grabis, J., Henkel, M., Jokste, L., Kampars, J., Koç, H., Kuhr, J.-C., Llorca, C., Loucopoulos, P., Juanes Pascual, R., Pastor, O., Sandkuhl, K., Simic, H., Stirna, J., Zdravkovic, J.: Capability driven development: an approach to designing digital enterprises. Bus. Inf. Syst. Eng. (BISE), **57**(1) (2015). doi:10.1007/s12599-014-0362-0
20. Henkel, M., Stratigaki, C., Stirna, J., Loucopoulos, P., Zorgios, Y., Migiakis, A.: Combining tools to design and develop software support for capabilities. Complex Syst. Inf. Model. Q., CSIMQ, (10), 38–52 (2017). https://doi.org/10.7250/csimq.2017-10.03

A Capability-Oriented Approach to IT Governance: The Case of Public Service Organizations

Jelena Zdravkovic[1(✉)] and Irina Rychkova[2]

[1] Department of Computer and Systems Sciences, Stockholm University,
Postbox 7003, 164 07 Kista, Sweden
jelenaz@dsv.su.se
[2] Centre de Recherche en Informatique, Universtity Paris 1, Pantheon-Sorbonne, Paris, France
irina.rychkova@univ-paris1.fr

Abstract. Getting more value from IT is becoming a critical objective for today's organizations. IT Governance is an important strategic instrument that should ensure organizations to succeed with this objective and therefore it needs to be efficiently planned, structured and executed. To respond to increasing service demands while preserving or even increasing the value provided by services, public organizations require resources and abilities that lay outside their boundaries - such as co-production, open innovation, as well as engagement of citizens and partner organizations. To respond to these challenges, public organizations need to employ new governance solutions to their IT to overcome the shortcomings of hierarchical structures and traditional centralized decision-making. In this study, we discuss a capability-oriented governance approach, which aligns envisioned public values with actors, processes and resources and accordingly compound different IT Governance capabilities. We illustrate our proposal on the student mobility case in the Higher Education public service.

Keywords: Capability · Public organisation · Public value · IT Governance

1 Introduction

Information technologies are evolving in business use at an endlessly increasing extent - e-Government, distance/hybrid education, e-Health, e-Commerce, e-collaboration, are just few examples of influential applications, which shape strategies in both private and public business sector. Getting more value from IT is an increasingly important organizational competency [2]; in this context, IT Governance is an instrument aimed to ensure that business organizations will meet their strategic goals.

IT Governance is a part of corporate governance, focused on specifying the decision rights and accountability framework to encourage desirable behavior in using IT [2]. In [2], the authors emphasize the importance of IT Governance in organizations as an integral part of the corporate governance. The purpose of IT Governance concerns overseeing design and implementation of processes, structures and relational mechanisms in organizations to enable both business- and IT people to execute their responsibilities

© Springer International Publishing AG 2017
A. Metzger and A. Persson (Eds.): CAiSE 2017 Workshops, LNBIP 286, pp. 39–49, 2017.
DOI: 10.1007/978-3-319-60048-2_4

in support of Business/IT alignment as well as the creation of business value from IT-enabled business investments.

In this study, we examine IT Governance in the context of public organizations. The values of public organizations are notably associated with important social outcomes and require therefore long-term strategies and strong commitments in all their operational areas, including IT. Whereas opportunities are limitless, resources are scarce, and operations' complexities are growing. In order to be successful in creating values from their IT, modern public organizations have to ensure continuous engagement of beneficiaries (citizens) into setting the objectives for the IT and evaluation of the results as well as continuous engagement of partner organizations (co-producers) into standard creation and use [1, 3].

Meeting these requirements is challenging due to inherently hierarchical structure of public organizations and centralized decision making that also applies to their IT management. Whereas efficient in closed and stable business environments, centralized decision making shows serious drawbacks in open environments driven by innovations. Modern public organizations need to become a part of dynamic innovative ecosystem where they co-create value with citizens, government, policy-makers, as well as with other public and private organizations and institutions. To succeed in their missions, public organizations need to master governance styles to overcome the shortcomings of hierarchical structures and centralized decision-making.

Public value describes the value that an organization contributes to society. For public organizations, it is the value developed for individual citizens, communities and organizations through provisioning of services, including lately increasing extent of online services enabled by IT. Thus, we consider public value as a foundational concept for structuring of IT Governance in the public sector. Furthermore IT-enabled value creation heavily depends on the organizational context – for effectively designing IT Governance structures, processes and relational mechanisms, public organizations need to define the context of IT Governance, which aside from organization's value is influenced by its core functionalities, involved authorities, legislations, and other.

In this research study, *we consider IT Governance as an organizational capability.* The interest in reasoning about IT Governance in an organization in terms of capabilities is twofold: (a) capability can operationalize the value from IT by defining the ability for delivering this value by compounding context-specific relevant behaviors in using IT; (b) capability can support configurability, re-use and mapping of IT Governance structures, processes and relational mechanisms in an organization.

The remainder of the paper is organized as follows: in Sect. 2 we present the relevant theoretical background; in Sect. 3 we describe our approach for structuring IT Governance as capability, and in Sect. 4 we illustrate these results on a case of the Higher Education sector. Section 5 provides discussion, concluding remarks and directions of future work.

2   Background

2.1   Organizational Styles

The terms centralization and decentralization often refer to the points of power over the decisions made in an organization. According to [4], when all the power for decision making rests at a single point in the organization ("center") - the structure should be called *centralized*; when the power is dispersed among many organizational entities, the structure should be called *decentralized*; when decision making is shared between the center and the other organizational entities, then the structure is *federated*.

Centralized organizations are very stable and robust but they cannot respond easily to change and are typically slow in acting. This also applies to their IT. Following [4, 5], we summarize the following reasons for decentralization in IT:

– Decision-making powers need to be shared. Power has to be placed where the knowledge is.
– Innovation through IT requires an extreme agility from organizations. Making decisions locally improves agility and reduces time needed to address the issue.
– Creative people require considerable room for maneuver. Resistance to new technologies due to the lack of understanding or fear to put at risk the existing position often comes from the center and jeopardizes new opportunities.

2.2   IT Governance in Public Organizations

For implementing IT Governance, an organization has to identify the scope of IT and the main areas/issues where decisions have to be made. The organization has to define its decision-making structures (i.e., organizational units, specific roles, committees) responsible for making these IT decisions; it has to design and implement processes for IT decision-making and IT monitoring to ensure the desired behaviors using IT; eventually, it has to specify the mechanisms supporting the active participation of, and collaborative relationship among entities appointed to defined governance structures [1, 2].

Over the years, a number of IT Governance frameworks have emerged, such as ISO 38500 [6] and COBIT [7]. In our study, we are not aiming to design a new framework but rather to consider reusable IT Governance solutions for different organizational styles ranging from centralized to decentralized types.

Centralized IT Governance fits when Business or IT monarchies are applied in most of decision areas [2]. This governance style is relevant when the high degree of standardization is required and cost-efficiency is one of the primary value sources. Federated IT Governance follows duopolies and federal governance structures. This style can be beneficial for organizations seeking for cost-efficient use of the assets, and at the same time, IT-enabled innovation. Decentralized IT Governance fits to the organizations focusing on innovation and time to market, and with the tendency to delegate decision making from the center to local units or project teams.

A modern public organization can be seen as a part of a dynamic ecosystem, where it maintains the relationships of different nature with other organizations and individuals (Fig. 1). To successfully achieve business goals in this complex environment, the organization needs to master different governance styles and use them according to a given context.

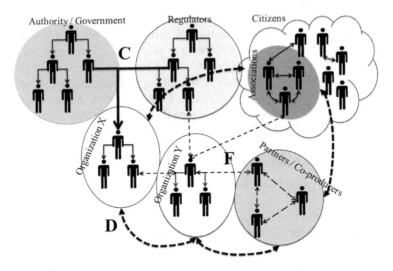

Fig. 1. Organizational ecosystem. C (centralized), D (decentralized) and F (federated) characterize the relationships between the organization and other parts of its environment.

2.3 Capability-Driven Approach

From the business perspective, *a capability describes what the business does that creates value for customers* [8]. It represents a design from a result-based perspective including various dimensions including organization's values, goals, processes, people, and resources. The notion is obtaining a growing presence in the business and IT alignment frameworks [9] starting from more business-oriented such as Business Architecture and Business Modeling, towards the alignment-oriented represented by Enterprise Architecture (EA), and Enterprise Modeling (EM). In brief, the emergence of the use of the capability notion seems having the following motivations:

- In the context of business planning, capability is becoming recognized as a fundamental component to describe what a core business does and, in particular, as an ability for delivering value, beneath the business strategy [8];
- Capability supports configurability of operations on a higher level than services and process, and according to changes in operational business context [10].

Following the above, we consider IT Governance capabilities as the abilities and capacities of an organization to ensure maximum value from its IT in a given context.

3   ITG Capability for Public Organizations

Public value describes how an organization contributes to society. Value for the public is a result of evaluations about how basic needs of individuals, groups and a society as a whole are addressed in relationships involving service provisioning [11]. Whereas private value is associated with satisfying individual desires, public value is mostly focused on achieving social outcomes. We generalize the findings of [12] on how IT investments generate public value and propose to distinguish between:

1. Value from delivering specific benefits directly to citizens
2. Value from improving an organization itself as a public asset

Each of these value types can be associated with one or multiple value sources: cost saving, increase in quality of service, enabling new services, and intrinsic enhancements (i.e., changing environment providing political, social, cultural impact, improving general quality of life of an individual or a group).

Public organizations are not free to choose their market - they are authorized to provide their services by their environment that involves government, employees, suppliers, local communities, citizens, policy makers, controlling organizations, etc. The authorizing environment provides the organizations with *legitimacy and support* and may vary depending on the scope of the IT project and its aimed value. For example, public organizations can be mandated by their authorizing environment to deliver a specific service, ensuring compliance with regulations, recommendations and standards.

Public organizations need to develop and manage their *core capabilities* in order to deliver results. Compared to private organizations, much of capacity required to produce public value lay outside the public organization and thus not under its direct control. To succeed in their missions, public organizations need not only to develop internal capabilities controlled by the organization itself, but also to explore co-production opportunities with external partners (e.g., other public and private organizations, volunteers, associations etc.) by means of external capabilities.

In our view, the three elements above together define an *IT Governance context* answering (a) what public value(s) the organization is seeking to produce by support of IT; (b) what sources of legitimacy and support will authorize, provide, or consume resources to create that value; and (c) which core capabilities are in place to deliver the main service of the organization.

For a given context, being determined by its three constituting elements, an ITG capability is used to specify what a public organization should be able to do to ensure support for that context by means of processes and resources, which in turn support organization's goals measured by KPIs (Key Performance Indicators). These indicators are also highly important for public organizations as their stakeholders (state, municipalities, citizens and other) want to ensure that an implementation of IT delivers values, which can effectively be measured by corresponding KPI [13]. We have formalized the above outlined concepts and relationships in a model (Fig. 2, below).

- *Legitimacy (and Support)*: to whom the organization is authorized to provide its services and by whom it gets support.

- *Core Capabilities*: they are describing what the organization is essentially doing.
- *Public Values:* they describe how the organization aims to contribute to the society.
- *Context:* it represents the information that can be used to characterize the situational environment of a public organization. The context of an IT Governance capability is defined by analyzing the *public value* the organization aims to create, its sources of *legitimacy and support* and *core capabilities*, which eventually lead to the goals to be achieved and the processes and resources to support the goals.
- *Goal:* it is a desired state of affairs, which needs to be attained to realize established value. Goals can be refined into sub-goals forming a goal model refining desired behaviors in using IT, such as cost-effective use of IT, or effective use of IT for growth; and effective use of IT for business flexibility.
- *Key Performance Indicator (KPI)*: it is a measurable property that can be seen as a target for achievement of a Goal.
- *Actor:* it is a person or even a part of the organization holding the responsibility for the achievement of a goal; for IT Governance, these actors may be organization's executives, IT decision makers, etc.
- *Process:* it is a series of actions that are performed in order to support one or more of the established goals. In the IT Governance domain the processes concern decision making about IT, coordination of IT processes, IT monitoring, performance management and other.
- *Resource:* When initiated, a process is perceived to engage or consume resources - people, materials, software. IT Governance processes rely for example on the actors involved in IT decision-making enactment and monitoring, as well as on the needed entities – technology and infrastructure supporting processes' execution, as well as coordination and communication between involved actors.

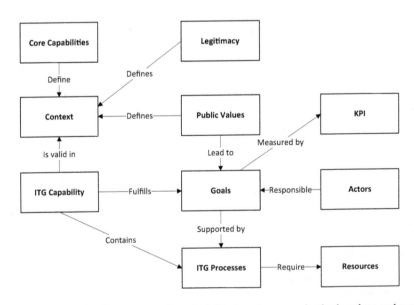

Fig. 2. A model for IT Governance using capability based on organization's values and context

- *IT Governance Capability*: it is ability and capacity of to ensure maximum value from its IT in a given Context.

We explained in Sect. 2.1 that organizations may follow different organizational styles, where centralized, federated and decentralized are the essential; in addition, new styles are emerging. In [14] we have proposed different IT Governance solutions using the capability notion to fit each of the organizational styles to obtain the patterns that could be applied in concrete cases for forming adequate IT Governance structure. This study differs in the way that we here elaborate a case from the public sector (student mobility, see Sect. 4) for which the IT Governance capability pattern for the federated organization style applies (Table 1):

Table 1. Capability pattern: *federated IT Governance, public sector*

Context	*Using IT for improving the organization:* value comes from improving efficiency and effectiveness of the organization itself (e.g., cost saving, improved processes, enabling new internal services), resulting in reputation and public opinion *Using IT for delivering direct benefit to a customer or to a community:* value sources include improving user experience from the existing services, enabling new services for citizens, enabling cooperation opportunities and partnerships for other organizations, and broader impact on the society via intrinsic enhancements *Government*, controlling organizations and *policy makers* are the main client of the program/project. They authorize the program/project and support it in a form of appropriate recommendations, laws, directives, standards Example: mobile and radio communication standards, regulations on privacy/security *Communities and citizens* indirectly evaluate the outcomes expressing their opinion about the organization as a whole
Goals	*Cost-effective use of IT; Effective use of IT for asset utilization; Effective use of IT for growth; High process integration; Centralized data management*
KPIs	*Measures of the Goals;* IT cost/total cost, Number of processes integrated, Centralized data/all data
Actors	IT Governance structures follow duopoly, feudal and federated archetypes – the relevant actors are: *C-level executives, Representatives from authority, Project Leaders (internal and external), IT and domain experts (internal and external), Representatives from controlling organizations*
Processes	*IT performance measurement based on KPIs, SLAs, Processes for conflict resolution between local control (at co-producers) and global control (organization and authority), Coordination between the central and local production, Semi-formal processes for communication and coordination on the horizontal level (focused groups, discussions, communities of practice) supported by technology*
Resources	*Internal production and co-production based on shared resources* (knowledge, technology, infrastructure, services): *Infrastructure and solutions supporting coordination within and between levels* (i.e., groupware, social networks); Standard solutions providing centralized reporting, Business Intelligence, ERP, CRM, SCM
ITG capability	Organizational IT plays the role of a mediator (service bus), coordinating and controlling the inter-organizational processes between partners. The organization itself provides the standards to ensure coordination/communication between co-producers. It also links the co-producers with the end users (citizens)

4   Example Case - Enabling Student Mobility with IT

Universities (including the ones the authors of this paper work for) show an increasing need to adjust governance of their IT according to the organizational structure and decision-making in place. In this example, we focus on the Federated IT Governance style and its corresponding capabilities.

The Erasmus Programme (European Region Action Scheme for the Mobility of University Students) is a European Union (EU) student exchange programme established in 1987 (see also Wikipedia/Erasmus Programme). Erasmus students can spend between one and three academic years in another European country studying or making an internship in another (host) university. Universities in Sweden and France are actively involved in Erasmus mobility. The aimed public value is to improve service quality and to enable new opportunities for universities, students and communities. Co-creation of value with partners from other organizations (universities) is required in this context.

One of the basic rights each exchange student has is the full recognition of courses passed successfully abroad by the home university. Before leaving the home university, a participating student signs the Learning Agreement - a document that describes the programme of studies followed in the host university. At the end of the stay, the host university prepares for the student a document called Transcript of Records, which confirms the completed studies' programme and the results. These documents are the legally binding for all parties involved (i.e. the home and host university). Should a student face problems in recognition, the student can seek a help of student organizations to make the courses validated [15].

In practice, Erasmus requires a tight coordination between university international department, university administration, faculty administration and European authorities. The following issues illustrate the need of flexible yet explicit IT Governance mechanisms for supporting Erasmus program at the universities:

Course planning
Learning agreement typically allows a student to choose courses from different master programs, different levels of study (e.g., master of the first or second year) sometimes even offered by different university departments. Planning the courses while allowing maximum flexibility for exchange students require a tight collaboration and coordination between different administration levels and departments at the involved universities.

Grading and grade mapping
Different approaches to education, cultural specifics, language and local grading systems are hard to merge and to map to single objective evaluation greed. Even though the Bologna system offers one, it needs to be adjusted locally, according to the university and country specifics.

To ensure comparable, compatible and coherent systems of Higher Education, the partners (co-producers) need to comply with Bologna Process [16]. This compliance requires significant changes in the organizational IT. Therefore, the sources of legitimacy and support in this context include university authorities and policy makers on the country and European level (for Bologna Process). This context reveals that the federated IT Governance is the most relevant (Table 1, the previous section). When implementing the federated IT Governance capability pattern presented in Table 2, organizational IT plays the role of a mediator, coordinating and controlling the inter-organizational processes between partners. It also links the (partner) universities with the students. Data integration between universities and standards for data exchange are of a main interest. The actors include university international office, head of faculties, program managers, faculty members, IT department. The processes and the resources supporting the main service are standardized, and controlled by the European representatives and university authorities in order to ensure the compliance.

Table 2. Instantiating Federated IT Governance pattern for supporting student mobility

Context	Value comes from efficient processes and services for managing mobility programs: e.g., providing the incoming students with accommodation, insurance, transport cards, easy access to the university facilities, language courses, etc. Coordination and planning the curricula, providing supporting material in English if the courses are in local language etc. Internal services for course planning if an incoming student selects modules from different programs/departments/faculties University administration, faculty administration, European level authorities can be considered as the main client of the Erasmus mobility programme. They authorize the program and support it in a form of appropriate standards (i.e., Bologna agreement) Communities and citizens indirectly evaluate the outcomes expressing their opinion about the organization (i.e. University) as a whole
Goals	High process compliance and integration and centralized data management in order to ensure compliance with Bologna and seamless coordination/communication with partner universities (host universities – home universities)
KPIs	Number of processes integrated, Number of compliant processes, Centralized data/all data
Actors	The relevant actors are: European committees for higher education, Erasmus coordinators on European, country and university levels, faculty administration, representatives from controlling organizations
Processes	IT performance measurement based on KPIs, SLAs, Processes for conflict resolution between local control Universities and faculties) and global control (universities, European level organizations), Coordination between the central and local production following Bologna; Semi-formal processes for communication and coordination between universities, translating and mapping the academic records according to Bologna rules etc. (many issues are solved case-based, between local program coordinators, by e-mail)
Resources	Internal production and co-production based on shared resources (knowledge, technology, infrastructure, services): Infrastructure and solutions supporting coordination within and between levels (our experience shows very weak automation so far)
ITG capability	Organizational IT (i.e. the host- and home university student management systems) plays the role of a mediator (service bus), coordinating and controlling the inter-organizational processes between partners. It also links the (partner) universities with the students

5   Discussion, Conclusions and Future Work

Values created by public organizations and their IT in particular, expand the boundaries of these organizations. Therefore, today's public organizations need to be seen as a part of dynamic ecosystems, where they maintain the relationships of different nature with individuals and other organizations. To fulfill their goals, public organizations need to adapt to their context, exhibiting consequently various behavior in using IT.

Next, the organization needs to examine its context: what public value it desires to provide, what its authorizing environment is (i.e., who will authorize and support the value provisioning, who will benefit from it), and, eventually, what kind of core organizational capabilities will be required. These elements are interrelated and provide an understanding of a context where the IT Governance will be enacted. We suggested that the model of IT Governance could become "more centralized" or "more decentralized" according to this context. We therefore considered IT Governance as an organizational capability and proposed to use IT Governance capability patterns for different organizational styles. An IT Governance capability pattern can be seen as a guideline on how to define IT governance to support desired public values driving different context situations. We illustrated how the IT Governance patterns can be instantiated on the case of the student mobility in the Higher Education public sector of EU. Our motivating assumption has been that public organizations need to master a wide range of ITG mechanisms and to deploy them depending on their value-creation context.

The model proposed in Fig. 2 provides an organizing logic that can help organizations to position, justify and govern their IT projects in a consistent way, based on the public value concept. However, argue that the IT Governance styles are not mutually exclusive and that several styles can be used in the same value-creation context. We plan to elaborate the guidelines and recommendations further in the future, by conducting multiple empirical studies and collaborating with practitioners. IT Governance capability patterns are intended to facilitate the application of IT Governance mechanisms for different governance styles. They provide a general idea; the concrete "recipe" has to be elaborated for each particular organization.

References

1. Weill, P., Ross, J.W.: IT Governance: How Top Performers Manage it Decision Rights for Superior Results. Harvard Business School Press, Boston (2004). ISBN 978-3-319-14547-1
2. De Haes, S., Van Grembergen, W.: Enterprise Governance of Information Technology. Springer, New York (2015). ISBN 978-3-319-14547-1
3. Moore, M.H.: Creating Public Value: Strategic Management in Government. Harvard University Press, Cambridge (1997). ISBN 9780674175587
4. Mintzberg, H.: The Structuring of Organizations: A Synthesis of the Research. University of Illinois at Urbana-Champaign's Academy for Entrepreneurial Leadership Historical Research Reference in Entrepreneurship (1979)
5. Morgan, J.: The Future of Work: Attract New Talent, Build Better Leaders, and Create a Competitive Organization. Wiley, Hokoken (2014). ISBN 978-1-118-87724-1
6. ISO 38500. Governance of IT for the Organization. https://webstore.iec.ch/preview/info_isoiec38500%7Bed2.0%7Den.pdf. Accessed 5 Feb 2017

7. COBIT. Control Practices: Guidance to Achieve Control Objective for Successful IT Governance. http://www.isaca.org/Knowledge-Center/Research/ResearchDeliverables/Pages/COBIT-Control-Practices-Guidance-to-Achieve-Control-Objective-for-Successful-IT-Governance-2nd-Edition.aspx. Accessed 15 Jan 2017

8. Ulrich, W., Rosen, M.: The Business Capability Map: Building a Foundation for Business/IT Alignment. Cutter Consortium for Business and Enterprise Architecture (2016). http://www.cutter.com/content-and-analysis/resource-centers/enterprise-architecture/sample-our-research/ea110504.html. Accessed 28 Feb 2016

9. Zdravkovic, J., Stirna, J., Grabis, J.: A comparative analysis of using the capability notion for congruent business- and information systems engineering. Complex Syst. Inf. Model. Q., CSIMQ, 10, 1–20 (2017). https://doi.org/10.7250/csimq.2017-10.01

10. Bērziša, S., et al.: Capability driven development: an approach to designing digital enterprises. Bus. Inf. Syst. Eng. (BISE) **57**(1) (2015). doi:10.1007/s12599-014-0362-0

11. Meynhardt, T.: public value inside: what is public value creation? Int. J. Public Admin. **32**(3–4), 192–219 (2009)

12. Cresswell, A.M., Burke, B., Pardo, T.: Advancing return on investment, analysis for government IT: a public value framework. Center for Technology in Government, University at Albany, SUNY (2006)

13. Mueller, L., et al.: IBM IT Governance Approach Business Performance through IT Execution. IBM Red Books (2008). http://www.redbooks.ibm.com/redbooks/pdfs/sg247517.pdf

14. Rychkova, I., Zdravkovic, J.: Towards decentralized IT governance in the public sector: a capability-oriented approach. In: Information Technology Governance in Public Organizations – Theory and Practice. Integrated Series in Information Systems, Springer, Heidelberg (2017, accepted)

15. Erasmus+Programme (2017). https://esn.org/Erasmus. Accessed 10 Feb 2017

16. Bologna Process. In: Wikipedia, The Free Encyclopedia, 10 June 2016. https://en.wikipedia.org/w/index.php?title=Bologna_Process&oldid=724628455

COGNISE 2017 – Cognitive Aspects of Information Systems Engineering

Using Visual Notations with Modeling Experts or Novices: What do the Experts Think?

Dirk van der Linden[✉]

Department of Information Systems, University of Haifa, Haifa, Israel
djtlinden@is.haifa.ac.il

Abstract. This short paper addresses the question of whether practitioners perceive requirements for the cognitive effectiveness of a visual notation to have different importance when that visual notation is used with modeling experts (i.e., developers, modelers) and novices (i.e., business stakeholders, end-users). Through analysis of data resulting from an ongoing empirical study we show that some requirements differ in how important they are perceived for modeling expert and novice use, but that these differences are difficult to meaningfully assess without further in-depth qualitative work.

Keywords: Conceptual modeling · Visual notation · Requirements · Expert–novice

1 Introduction

It is important that the visual notations of conceptual models used in development processes communicate their intended meaning effectively and correctly: that they are *cognitively effective* [2]. With the multitude of stakeholders involved in a typical information system development process, many of them will likely have little to no modeling expertise. This leads to an expert–novice distinction that should be kept in mind while creating diagrams to be shown to such non-modeling expert stakeholders [6].

This expert–novice distinction has been noted widely in literature [4], as well the positive effect that training has on the correct grasping of information contained in diagrams [1]. Theory on cognitively effective design for visual notations tells us that representation ought to be tailored to different users and media [5], noting in particular the following expert–novice differences:

- Novices have more difficulty discriminating between symbols.
- Novices are more affected by complexity as they lack "chunking" strategies.
- Novices have to consciously remember what symbols mean.

This paper treats the following research questions: *(i) do modeling experts weigh requirements for cognitively effective design differently if models are intended for use with non-experts?*, and if so, *(ii) do these differences reflect the expert–novice differences noted by [5]?*

© Springer International Publishing AG 2017
A. Metzger and A. Persson (Eds.): CAiSE 2017 Workshops, LNBIP 286, pp. 53–58, 2017.
DOI: 10.1007/978-3-319-60048-2_5

2   Empirical Study

The data we use here result from an ongoing study into the requirements that practitioners who employ conceptual modeling techniques in their daily practice have towards visual notations [3]. This study consists of a questionnaire set out via LinkedIn Professional Groups, targeting practitioners working in relevant fields, e.g., software engineering/architecture, requirements engineering, enterprise engineering/architecture, business analysis.

The questionnaire consists of three parts, (i) demographic data, (ii) qualitative elicitation of modeling purpose & foci, and (iii) quantitative weighting of requirements for cognitively effective visual notations. Here we focus on iii. To assess whether modeling experts weigh requirements (as given by the Physics of Notations [5]) differently when using them with modeler experts or novices, we posed the following question, followed by having participants rate these requirements on a 5 points Likert scale ranging from not important at all to very important. *"Suppose that for your modeling efforts you would be able to have an ideal visual notation, suited especially to your purposes. You would be using this notation only among fellow modeling experts. On a scale of 1 to 5, how important would the following requirements be for this notation? It should..."*

- have a 1:1 correspondence between semantic constructs and graphical symbols (semiotic clarity, SemCla)
- clearly distinguish between different symbols (perceptual discriminability, PerDis)
- use visual representations whose appearance suggests their meaning (semantic transparency, SemTra)
- have explicit mechanisms for dealing with complexity (complexity management, CogMan)
- have explicit mechanisms to support integration of information from different diagrams (cognitive integration, CogInt)
- use the full range and capacity of visual variables such as shape, color, size, etc. (visual expressiveness, VisExp)
- use text to complement graphics (dual coding, DuaCod)
- have no more than a cognitively manageable number of different graphical symbols (graphic economy, GraEco)
- use different visual dialects for different tasks and audiences (cognitive fit, CogFit)

After rating each item, participants were asked *"are there any requirements you feel are not covered by the ones you just saw, specific to the use of a visual notation among fellow modeling experts?"*. We then repeated the weighting with the same items, but posed the question for modeling novices, by noting "You would be using this notation also with other stakeholders that have no expertise in modeling, such as business experts or end-users."

3   Findings

The findings are based on an initial sample of 84 participants. In Fig. 1 the distribution of scores for each requirement are shown, divided into using models with (a) experts, and (b) novices.

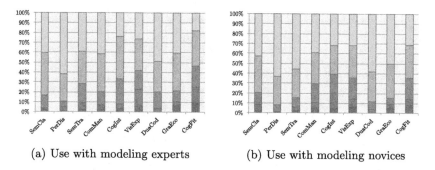

(a) Use with modeling experts   (b) Use with modeling novices

Fig. 1. Comparison of polarities ratios for each requirement. From top to bottom the different colors represent the range of very important to not important at all. (Color figure online)

On a first glance there seem to be differences in how modeling experts weigh these requirements. To compare the two sets of responses, we show the median scores for each requirement in Fig. 2. The median scores for requirements when models are used with modeling experts (XP) and modeling novices (nXP) differ only (slightly, 0.5 to 1) for three principles: (i) semantic transparency, (ii) dual coding, and (iii) graphic economy.

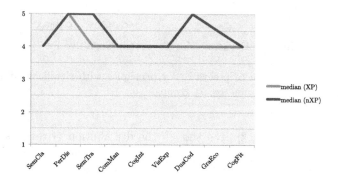

Fig. 2. Median scores (1–5) for each PoN principle ($n = 84$).

To check more clearly whether there are differences between the expert and non-expert answers, we used Wilcoxon signed rank testing to assess how distinct each requirement pair is. Four principles gave significant ($p < 0.05$) difference, namely semantic transparency ($p = 0.0054$), visual expressiveness ($p = 0.0477$), graphic economy ($p = 0.04036$), and cognitive fit ($p = 0.00142$). However, to interpret these findings, we need to look at the actual distributions of answers for these requirements, shown in Fig. 3.

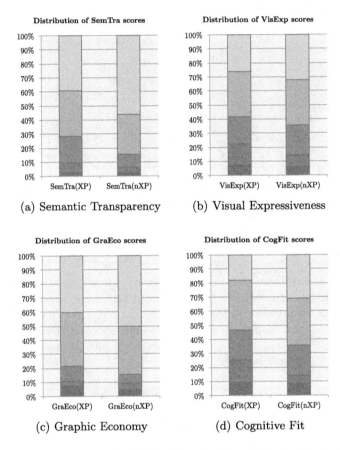

Fig. 3. Detailed comparison of polarities for principles with significant difference in median between expert and non-expert groups.

As can be seen in Fig. 3, even though the distribution of responses differs, whether it does so meaningfully is debatable. For example, semantic transparency, the use of visual representations whose appearance suggests their meaning, is considered important by ≈70% of participants when used with only modeling experts. This rises to ≈85% when used with modeling novices. Whether a difference of 15% constitutes a significant enough difference to answer research question (i) *do modeling experts weigh requirements for cognitively effective design differently if models are intended for use with non-experts?* requires more consideration, incorporating more qualitative research to assess how important such differences are perceived to be.

For research question (ii), *do these differences reflect the expert–novice differences noted by* [5]*?* the data seems to both hint affirmatively and contradict itself. The requirements in Fig. 3 are linked to the expert/novice distinction, as optimizing a visual 'dialect' of sorts for e.g., a novice user (cognitive fit) involves [5] involves restricting visual vocabulary size (graphic economy), ensuring graphical symbols suggest meaning (semantic transparency), and the use of visually expressive symbols. However, the noted importance of dealing with complexity as novices lack chunking strategies is not clearly reflected in the data, although the difference between expert and novice results for this requirement was just above the threshold of statistic significance ($p = 0.06148$).

4   Thoughts

When looking purely at the quantitative data resulting from this study so far, there does not seem to be a significant meaningful difference in how important the different requirements are perceived depending on the audience affected. As noted, likely the qualitative data analysis is required to fully assess the significance and meaning of these results. For example, when we asked participants to elaborate on any missed requirements, several responses dealt with re-emphasizing what is most important to them. These, albeit individual responses, paint a different color than the quantitative analysis above. For example, one participant noted:

> "I cannot do the formal models without'artist impressions' or rich pictures tailored to specific stakeholders or stakeholder groups, even fellow modeling insiders/experts."

This can be interpreted in at least two ways. First, that models should indeed be designed differently depending on the stakeholder group used, or the stage of development - in line with the need to accommodate expert–novice differences in visual notation design. Second, that before models are created, different representations altogether should be used for e.g., requirements elicitation and stakeholder alignment, before any capturing of information is done in conceptual models. This would negate, or at least severely reduce the need for expert–novice differences in visual representation, as the conceptual models would no longer be used with those stakeholders that are novices in modeling.

On the other hand, another participant noted the importance of having visual representation tailored to different stakeholders as well, but related it specifically to modeling languages:

> "Highlight how important is to have flexibility to communicate to several audiences perhaps incorporating a more complex visual design. The simplicity of the visual design of UML could be perfect for a software engineer but very cold for a Business User."

Here, we find more of a hint towards the need to have meaningful variability in the visual representation of the modeling languages – not different kinds representations altogether.

5 Concluding Outlook

This short paper discussed the importance, as perceived by modeling practitioners, of different requirements for cognitively effective visual notation design. We noted that, while in the quantitative findings there does not seem to be a clear distinction for how important these requirements are that links with expert/non-expert distinction, the qualitative findings of the same study can be used to contextualize them more meaningfully.

Thus, for further work on this study we will assess the outcomes of the quantitative data specifically in context of the findings resulting from the qualitative data. In particular, it seems that to get clear answers for whether modeling languages ought to support variability or differentiation for the expert–novice distinction we need to incorporate more qualitative studies, such as in-depth interviews with selected practitioners.

A consideration on the limitations discussed here can be that the limited differentiation in scores of some requirements reflect their, perhaps, ambiguous descriptions, and general counter-intuitive nature. For example, while most people will intuitively understand what it means that a graphical symbol suggests its meaning, and that adding more symbols leads to more complexity, requirements such as 'have explicit mechanisms to support integration of information from different diagrams' are less simple to understand at a first glance. However, in order to elicit a large dataset from practitioners, it is necessary to keep average answering time for the questionnaire down, making it difficult to present more details or examples.

References

1. DeSanctis, G., Jarvenpaa, S.L.: Graphical presentation of accounting data for financial forecasting: an experimental investigation. Acc. Organ. Soc. **14**(5–6), 509–525 (1989)
2. Larkin, J.H., Simon, H.A.: Why a diagram is (sometimes) worth ten thousand words. Cogn. Sci. **11**(1), 65–100 (1987)
3. Linden, D., Hadar, I.: User involvement in applications of the PoN. In: Krogstie, J., Mouratidis, H., Su, J. (eds.) CAiSE 2016. LNBIP, vol. 249, pp. 109–115. Springer, Cham (2016). doi:10.1007/978-3-319-39564-7_11
4. Lohse, G.L., Biolsi, K., Walker, N., Rueter, H.H.: A classification of visual representations. Commun. ACM **37**(12), 36–50 (1994)
5. Moody, D.L.: The "physics" of notations: toward a scientific basis for constructing visual notations in software engineering. IEEE Trans. Software Eng. **35**(6), 756–779 (2009)
6. Narayanan, N.H., Hübscher, R.: Visual language theory: towards a human-computer interaction perspective. In: Marriott, K., Meyer, B. (eds.) Visual Language Theory, pp. 87–128. Springer, New York (1998)

An Observation Method for Behavioral Analysis of Collaborative Modeling Skills

Ilona Wilmont[1,2]([⊠]), Stijn Hoppenbrouwers[2], and Erik Barendsen[1]

[1] Institute for Computing and Information Sciences, Radboud University Nijmegen,
P.O. Box 9010, 6500 GL Nijmegen, The Netherlands
{i.wilmont,e.barendsen}@cs.ru.nl
[2] HAN University of Applied Sciences, P.O. Box 2217,
6802 CE Arnhem, The Netherlands
stijn.hoppenbrouwers@han.nl

Abstract. Process modeling skills are strongly subject to individual differences in cognitive abilities. However, we lack systematic methods to analyze how psychological mechanisms facilitating cognition influence modeling skills.

In this study, we develop a method for a more ecologically valid analysis of modeling behavior based on data from interviews, observations of modeling sessions and literature review. The data was analyzed in a bottom-up fashion and compared to existing models to construct a coding scheme, which was tested on four independent modeling sessions until theoretical saturation was achieved.

The resulting categories of Abstraction, Reasoning, Monitoring, Shifting, Working memory, Initiation and Planning were consistently applicable to real modeling sessions. Future research may analyze behavioral patterns within and across these categories to provide valuable insights in the psychological mechanisms of how practitioners use modeling skills and related cognitive processes.

Keywords: Process modeling · Abstraction · Executive control · Reasoning

1   Introduction

Process modeling is a cognitively challenging activity, strongly subject to individual differences in performance [6,12,20,25,27]. Nevertheless, to the best of our knowledge we currently have no systematic, objective way of analyzing the cognitive aspects of modeling skills as it occurs in the practice of IT. Recent lab evidence shows positive correlations between working memory capacity (WMC) and process modeling quality [16], but correlations can only be taken as incentives to further explore such facilitating mechanisms.

In this study, we pose the following research question: *Which variables are essential to observe in a method to analyze individual variability in cognitive skills in modeling sessions?* Our literature review has revealed a critical role for

A. Metzger and A. Persson (Eds.): CAiSE 2017 Workshops, LNBIP 286, pp. 59–71, 2017.
DOI: 10.1007/978-3-319-60048-2_6

abstraction, relational reasoning and executive control in modeling [27]. Compatible with [16], evidence suggests that WMC expresses itself through executive control [10,18] and is a critical facilitator of both abstraction [3] and reasoning [13]. In this study, we validate these results firstly by comparing the findings to the opinions of experienced modeling practitioners, and secondly by checking whether the findings can indeed be made observable in real modeling sessions. Finally, based on all our results, we develop an observation method for systematic analysis of modeling skills. This method should provide more insight in the context in which WMC is expressed by describing how reasoning, abstraction and executive control manifest themselves in relation to each other and in relation to the modeling process. This may give us insights in why modeling performance is so individually variable, and allow us to train weak modelers in the specific skills strong modelers exhibit most.

We begin by reviewing our key variables. Secondly, we describe our data collection process and how we integrated the results with existing models to create an observation scheme for behavioral analysis. Finally, we discuss implications for future research.

2 Abstraction

Abstraction is one of the most difficult and most important modeling skills [12,23,25]. The overarching term 'abstraction' refers to the process of performing mental operations and simulations on a set of related objects without the objects in question being present [19]. 'Abstraction' as a noun encompasses the static component: mental representations. 'Abstracting' as a verb relates to mental operations, such as instantiation and generalization, which can be applied to any mental representation on any level of abstraction. In modeling, domain comprehension on an abstract level improves performance [15]. Additionally, abstract comprehension encourages engagement in problem solving behaviors, such as testing the consequences of model facts, which in turn improves overall model quality [6].

Most of the literature focusing on quantifying abstraction has classified abstraction into different levels, based either on mental imagery triggered by the concept [8,22] or on observation of neural activation in response to semantic prompts and relational reasoning tests [3]. All level classifications begin with a highly *concrete* level, which is defined as a richly detailed mental copy of the real object. Then, there are two or three gradually more abstract levels: one or two *medium* levels of abstraction, which encompass generic names of objects allowing us to know what one means well enough to hold a comprehensible conversation, and a *high* level of abstraction which is devoid of most detail. When talking on this level, if one does not know concrete domain processes and underlying infrastructure, comprehension is impossible. [21] specifically mentions that goal and focus of abstraction levels shift as they change; each level of increased abstraction shows different details which serve to specify certain systemic functions.

3 Relational Reasoning

Relational reasoning is strongly associated with success in both modeling [6,15] and problem solving in general [2,25]. [4] defines relational reasoning as "the ability to consider relationships between multiple mental representations". In essence, it comprises the operational component of abstraction: mental operations one can perform to relate or modify abstract representations. One combines experience, input from peers and existing model concepts and relations to form new representations, through a process of understanding, integration and structuring. The final result should meaningfully convey the model's purpose. Some of the most prominently occurring reasoning processes in the literature, which we use as inspiration for our method, are making assumptions [1], drawing analogies [9], explaining [25], elaborating [2], making inferences [2], integrating [26], rephrasing [25], summarizing [11] and verifying [2].

4 Executive Control

Executive functions are a set of monitoring functions on one's own behavior, primarily focusing on control and coordination of responses to input which might originate from the environment or from one's own thoughts [14]. This is achieved through processes such as inhibitory control, switching, working memory updating and monitoring [18]. Executive functions lie at the heart of modeling. A modeler continuously engages in inhibition and switching as he performs such diverse tasks as deducing and testing hypotheses on how model elements interact [23,25]. He must interpret and comprehend this information, and match his own mental representation with what other modelers are saying and writing [6]. He must be able to switch between different levels of abstraction for viewing system structures, focus his attention on different aspects of the problem in scope and regulate and monitor his selection in case of multiple simultaneous inputs [21,27]. Moreover, modelers should not only monitor themselves, but also others as the discussion progresses [27]. At the end of the session, the modeler needs to relate the modeling goals and the users' needs to the model created to ensure final model quality [24].

For ecologically valid, behavioral assessment of executive functions, several models exist. The main concept they share is that the different dimensions of executive functioning are all facilitated by a common underlying cognitive process, such as working memory, which allows maintenance of a goal state, and active evaluation of the current state against that goal state, to take place continuously [18]. Examples are the Behavior Rating Inventory for Executive Functions (BRIEF) [7] and educational assessment methods [5,17]. The BRIEF focuses on both ecological and clinical assessment of behavior using the factors Behavioural Regulation (BR), Emotional Regulation (ER) and Metacognition (M), whereas the educational methods aim to assess the most important executive skills in education. A comparison of the models is shown in Table 1. It is worth noting that in [5], Sustained attention is explicitly differentiated from

Working memory to draw a distinction between maintaining focus and remembering and manipulating information on the short term. Both Time management and Goal-directed persistence are scales which are not formally measured by any method in existence, because they are hard to assess within the context of a single test. Nevertheless, in real settings such as education and modeling, these are essential skills that will directly contribute to task achievement.

Table 1. A comparison of executive function models.

BRIEF [7]	Dawson and Guare [5]	Meltzer et al. [17]
Inhibit (BR)	Response inhibition	–
Self-monitoring (BR)	–	Self-monitoring
–	Sustained attention	–
Emotional control (ER)	Emotional control	–
Shifting (ER)	Flexibility	Shifting
Initiate (M)	Task initiation	–
Working memory (M)	Working memory	–
Plan/organize (M)	Planning	Planning
Organization of materials (M)	Organization	Organizing
Task-monitoring (M)	Metacognition	–
–	Goal-directed persistence	Goal setting
–	Time management	Prioritizing

5   Method

We first conducted exploratory interviews with modeling experts to verify whether their notion of essential modeling skills matched with what theory suggested to be essential modeling skills. The interviews were analyzed in a bottom-up fashion, using aspects of grounded theory. Then, we observed modeling sessions in IT industry. A small sample of these sessions was analyzed for modeling skills in the same bottom-up way as the interviews. The results from both the observations and the interviews were compared to the executive control models discussed above, from which a pilot observation scheme resulted. This scheme was tested on four independent modeling sessions until theoretical saturation was achieved, and revised to create a final observation scheme.

5.1   Expert Interviews

Five semi-structured interviews were conducted with experienced modeling facilitators, of which one was female and four were male. The sample included IT architects with different specializations: an enterprise architect, a business architect and two application architects working for a Dutch bank. Also, a business engineer working for an international IT company was included to contribute the perspective of one who was also involved with implementing solutions. An interview guide was prepared with main questions and probes about how the interviewees experience the facilitation of modeling sessions, what they consider to be critical modeling skills, different types of stakeholder responses and how they deal with them. The researcher provided scenarios, such as 'what would you do if you notice a participant in your session who does not manage to follow along', to stimulate the interviewees to think about what they would do or consider most important in such cases. All interviews were audio-recorded, by consent of the interviewees. Free talking was encouraged, with the researcher only probing if further information was desired, or to keep the interviewees within scope.

The interviews were analyzed directly from the audio files with Atlas.ti, following a grounded theory approach. Transcription was bypassed because the essential meaning was conveyed by the broader discussion of topics, not via formulations on word level. Firstly, open coding was applied to the interviews. No specific unit of analysis was defined, codes were assigned to fragments of speech which the researcher considered representative for the code in question. A few examples of codes assigned to utterances (translated from Dutch) can be found in Table 2. After open coding, the codes were grouped during a phase of axial coding according to the emerging categories. Resulting codes were discussed with an experienced IT professional for extra validation.

5.2   Observations of Modeling Sessions

We included observational research in our study because real-life modeling is subject to many influences currently still unknown to us. For both codebook construction and testing for theoretical saturation, a total of seven modeling sessions were analyzed. One session took place at a Dutch bank and included an IT architect, a program director and a program manager. No video recordings were allowed but the researcher present wrote up one elaborate report immediately after the session, describing actions done by session participants. Codes were assigned to those actions, and to described responses by other participants. For example, the reported sentence of "MV immediately began pointing out errors in the Archimate model, mostly pertaining to teams that no longer existed or had been merged" was coded as *error monitoring*.

The other sessions took place over the course of three months as part of a larger IT project in a Dutch organization, active in the collective sector. The sessions included a business analyst, a project leader, an architect and a change manager. Camera and audio recordings were made with all participants' consent. A camcorder on a tripod was put up in a corner so that it would capture as much of the scene as possible, without it being too obtrusive for the participants. The researcher had been present at all sessions in a non-obtrusive manner. Before the observations, the researcher had met and talked with all participants to get to know them and get them accustomed to her presence. No interventions were done during the sessions. The observations took place at the organizations' offices,

Table 2. Examples of codes assigned to utterances during the interviews.

Utterance	Code	Rationale
"we say okay, assume you are leading a discussion about how you as a company will put your products in the market, will you talk about the distribution channels, you talk about how you produce it"	INSTANTIATE	The interviewee describes the concept of how to put products on the market and gives more concrete examples, or instances, of how to do this: via distribution channels or the way you produce the product
"that you went through it properly yourself, that you took out the essence and that in advance, you shortly present 'this is it … this is what I want to discuss with you and eh … to then go through the material for an hour max"	ABSTRACT ESSENTIAL MEANING	The interviewee talks about how to prepare for a session: being immersed in the details of the situation and having abstracted the essence of it so that he is well prepared for which key points to discuss
"you have to follow a very strict line when you begin to denote things … on the other hand you have to learn to let go because the danger of modeling is that it becomes some kind of dogma"	SCOPE MONITORING	The interviewee talks about the difficulty of guarding scope on the one hand, both with regard to what to denote and how to denote it in a model, and on the other hand giving participants some freedom so that new interesting issues might emerge

and were typically rooms with whiteboards and brown paper sheets attached to the walls. Participants were free to make sketches and notes in this way. The final products were photographed, and resulting digital documentation was also collected.

The recorded sessions were fully transcribed. We directly coded the utterances of all participants using a grounded theory approach with Atlas.ti. A phase of open coding was followed by two cycles of axial coding. During open coding, the unit of analysis was a participant's full turn, terminated only by an interruption or a natural reaction from another participant. Pauses between speech but still continued by the same participant were taken to belong to a single turn unless they exceeded 10 s. In addition to the emerging codes, each turn was specifically assigned a level of abstraction, to monitor the flow of abstraction levels throughout the discussion. A certain amount of bias in formulating codes resulted from the literature study on executive functions, but additionally, many new codes were formulated which did not appear as such in existing literature. An example of a coded fragment (translated from Dutch) can be found in Table 3.

Table 3. Examples of codes assigned to a discussion fragment during the observations.

Who	Utterance	Codes	Rationale
M2	"we do not achieve the goal of the process, then we can very easily say that we change the goal of the process"	REASONING: INFERENCE; SWITCH: PROPOSE ALTERNATIVE; MONITOR: MONITOR GOAL; ABSTRACTION LEVEL: ABSTRACT	In this fragment, M2 makes an if-then inference, proposes the alternative of changing the goal of the process, but is at the same time monitoring the process goal by bringing the discussion to goal awareness. Finally, this statement is made in very abstract terms such as 'goal' and 'process'. We do not know exactly what details are encompassed in this
M1	"no but maybe we should also mention the outcome of the process . . . so to say, what is the most complete input the process can receive? What output is possible from this process? Well, complete eh . . . complete and timely registered income information . . . goal can also be that we do not register them in the end"	MONITOR: TEST PROPOSITION; SWITCH: PROPOSE ALTERNATIVE; ABSTRACTION: INSTANTIATE; ABSTRACTION LEVEL: ABSTRACT; ABSTRACTION LEVEL: MEDIUM	This utterance proposes first of all an alternative to the goal problem pointed out by M2 in the previous utterance. Also, M1 tries to test his proposition by making his notion of output more specific. This is immediately an instantiation, an act of abstracting to gain better understanding. He starts on an abstract level and lowers it to a medium level, on which we know more about the output but still not on a level of detail that talks about tangible, visual objects
M2	"yes but then we have a completely different goal . . . and this one . . . has nothing to do with the registration of income information"	MONITORING: INCONSISTENCY DETECTION; MONITORING: MONITOR GOAL; REASONING: INFERENCE; ABSTRACTION LEVEL: ABSTRACT	Here M2 makes the inconsistency with M1's notion of output and the modeling goal explicit, hence both the inconsistency detection and the goal monitoring codes. He also makes an inference by implying that if M1's notion is true, then they have a goal problem. He still talks on an abstract level about goals and income information

6 Results

After categorizing the emerging codes from both the interviews and the observations, we compare the categories emerging from interviews and observation to those found in the literature to construct a pilot observation scheme.

6.1 Pilot Observation Scheme

An overview of the resulting categories and codes obtained from the interviews and the observations compared to the assessment items provided by existing schemes described in the literature is provided in Table 4.

Table 4. A comparison of the categories from the interviews, observations and literature study.

Interviews	Observations	Literature	Pilot scheme
Goal-directedness	Goal-directedness	Goal-directed persistence	**Goal-directedness**
Initiation/ exploration	Initiation	Task initiation	**Initiation**
Maintaining attention	Working memory	Working memory/ sustained attention	**Working memory**
Mental flexibility	Switching	Flexibility/shifting	**Shifting**
Monitoring	Monitoring	Metacognition/ monitoring	**Monitoring**
–	Inhibition	Response inhibition	–
Reasoning processes	Reasoning	–	**Reasoning**
Abstraction	Abstraction	–	**Abstraction**
Communication/ people skills	–	–	–
Modeller characteristics	–	–	–
–	–	Time management	–
–	–	Organisation	–
–	–	Planning	–
–	–	Emotional control	–

The categories in the pilot scheme can be defined as follows:

- **Goal-directedness:** Any act relating to any goals of the modeling session. These can for example be modeling goals, planning goals or organizational goals.
- **Initiation:** Any act relating to the start of a new task or discuss a new topic.

- **Working memory:** Any act in which the modeler returns to a previously mentioned topic or repeats and manipulates previously mentioned information.
- **Shifting:** Any act relating to a switch in related topics or perspectives without deviating from the main focus.
- **Monitoring:** Any act relating to monitoring the progress of the session, the structure or content of the model, the way utterances are related to set goals, comprehension of other modelers, guarding discussion scope and error monitoring.
- **Reasoning:** Any process of considering multiple mental representations in relation to each other.
- **Abstraction:** Any act of observing processes in more detail to gain better understanding, or in less detail to gain better overview of the whole picture.

The categories of Goal-directedness, Initiation, Working memory, Shifting and Monitoring, appear in the interviews, observations and the literature. It thus seems justified to keep them as categories for the final coding scheme.

Response inhibition as measured by the items in the BRIEF or the educational models is extremely difficult to implement, as the educational models are tailored to children whose inhibitory control is still developing, and most of the BRIEF items, such as distractibility or impulsivity, are also not observable in modeling sessions. The only items which could be observed were if people broke off sentences halfway. This behavior appeared meaningless in the context of modeling, therefore we follow [17] and do not include inhibition as a separate category.

Reasoning and abstraction are both complex cognitive processes facilitated to a significant extent by executive functions, but are not considered executive functions themselves by existing measurement methods. In some studies, reasoning and abstraction are used as ways to observe executive function strength. They are both critical processes in modeling, and therefore we will include them in the coding scheme as the two main variables which will be examined in relation to the different executive functions.

Communication/People skills and Modeler characteristics were factors people only talked about in the interviews, when discussing their experiences from a generalized point of view. When observing sessions, such factors cannot be directly observed when the unit of analysis is defined as a single turn. There thus seems to be no reason to include them.

The factors Time management, Planning, Organization and Emotional control typically span an individual's functioning across a great many tasks. Within the context of a single modeling session, these factors were also not observable, and hence we have decided to exclude them from the final coding scheme.

6.2   Final Observation Scheme

We applied the pilot observation scheme to four further modeling sessions, taken from the same project, to achieve theoretical saturation.

Firstly, we found that coding Abstraction only in terms of concrete, medium and abstract levels did not capture the essence of the variable. For example, a modeler could be talking on a highly abstract level yet not be able to formulate the type of elegant solution that would solve a modeling problem. Therefore, we further refined Abstraction into *semantic* and *relational* abstraction, as in [3]. Semantic abstraction refers to the abstraction level of the words in an utterance, relational abstraction refers to the number of relations between the concepts discussed in an utterance. In this way, it became clear that, for example, semantically abstract concepts can be used in concrete relations, and that this, if not instantiated, can easily hide poor comprehension.

Secondly, we refined Reasoning into *comparative* and *transformative* reasoning processes. Transformative processes change the presentation of information, but preserve the essence of its meaning. It includes rephrasing and summarizing, but also instantiation and generalization, keeping the Abstraction category purely for classifying the abstraction level of an utterance. Comparative processes use two or more sources of input to derive some consequence for the next step in the reasoning process. Examples are inferencing, verifying, assuming and analogy. Furthermore, we merged codes which had significant semantic overlap and were indistinct in practice, such as *elaborate* and *explore*.

Thirdly, we found that aspects of communication, such as different forms of backchanneling, were after all critical to determine a modeler's initial reaction to a peer's utterances. We hence added Communication as a supportive category.

Finally, we found that goal-related utterances occur either within the context of a monitoring act, such as monitoring previously set process goals, or a planning act, such as articulating future session goals. Additionally, in these sessions another participant made heavy use of other planning aspects such as organizing modeling progress and articulating future actions. Therefore, we chose to eliminate Goal-directedness as an independent category, to add a Planning category into the coding scheme and to place the goal-related acts under both Monitoring and Planning.

The final coding scheme thus consists of the following categories (a full overview can be found on ilonawilmont.nl/codingscheme): Abstraction (*Semantic, Relational*), Reasoning (*Comparative, Transformative*), Initiation, Monitoring, Planning, Shifting, Working memory, Communication.

7   Discussion and Future Research

Our results strongly suggest that some aspects of executive control, in particular Monitoring and, to some extent, Shifting, are more clearly observable in this context than the more fundamental aspects such as Inhibition, Working memory and Emotional control. This does not mean that the fundamental processes do not play an important role, it simply shows that defects in the fundamental processes may no longer be so obvious in a working context as they might have been when they were still developing in a school setting. Nevertheless, this may be indicative of appropriate inhibition given the context. In future studies, we will therefore have to examine the relation between individual measures of both fundamental and metacognitive executive functions, abstraction and reasoning, and the behavioral patterns obtained through analysis with our method.

The scope of this study was limited to making observable abstraction, reasoning and executive control processes in a real modeling setting. In future work, we will analyze this data to come to actual patterns of modeling behavior. A potential technique for this is process mining. When assigning the quotations in Atlas.ti directly to the video fragment, one also has the duration of a cognitive process, and a process mining tool could then show how long people engage in certain cognitive processes, and how they consecutively follow up on each other. Analysis should also focus on the relations between the different categories and individual codes to understand the collaborative process of modeling. Which codes co-occur most frequently? What is the effect of this cluster of behaviors on other modelers in the session? Do they follow and continue the line of reasoning, or do they apply corrections?

Finally, at the current stage of research, we are left with the issue that we have no full inter-rater reliability score for the coding scheme. This will be resolved once we have applied the coding scheme to our full dataset of observations.

8   Conclusions

We have described how we have developed an observation method to analyze critical modeling skills, in particular abstraction, reasoning and certain executive control functions in real modeling sessions. We have compared results from expert interviews, observations and the extensive literature on abstraction, reasoning and executive control to construct an observation scheme. The resulting categories from the different data sources were remarkably consistent, of which Abstraction, Reasoning and Monitoring were most prominently present. Examination of the relations between codes and consecutively occurring groups of codes promises to provide insights in how psychological processes facilitate collaborative modeling.

References

1. Arthur, W.B.: Inductive reasoning and bounded rationality. Am. Econ. Rev. **84**(2), 406–411 (1994)
2. Chin, C., Brown, D.E.: Learning deeply in science: an analysis and reintegration of deep approaches in two case studies of grade 8 students. Res. Sci. Educ. **30**(2), 173–197 (2000)
3. Christoff, K., Keramatian, K., Gordon, A., Smith, R., Mdler, B.: Prefrontal organization of cognitive control according to levels of abstraction. Brain Res. **1286**, 94–105 (2009)
4. Crone, E.A., Wendelken, C., Van Leijenhorst, L., Honomichl, R.D., Christoff, K., Bunge, S.A.: Neurocognitive development of relational reasoning. Dev. Sci. **12**(1), 55–66 (2009)

5. Dawson, P., Guare, R.: Executive Skills in Children and Adolescents: A Practical Guide to Assessment and Intervention. Guilford Press, New York (2010)
6. Gemino, A., Wand, Y.: Evaluating modeling techniques based on models of learning. Commun. ACM **46**(10), 79–84 (2003)
7. Gioia, G.A., Isquith, P.K., Retzlaff, P.D., Espy, K.A.: Confirmatory factor analysis of the Behavior Rating Inventory of Executive Function (BRIEF) in a clinical sample. Child Neuropsychol. **8**(4), 249–257 (2002)
8. Goldstein, K., Scheerer, M.: Abstract and concrete behavior: an experimental study with special tests. Psychol. Monogr. **53**(2), 1–151 (1941)
9. Green, A.E., Fugelsang, J.A., Kraemer, D.J.M., Dunbar, K.N.: The micro-category account of analogy. Cognition **106**(2), 1004–1016 (2008)
10. Kane, M.J., Conway, A.R., Hambrick, D.Z., Engle, R.W.: Variation in working memory capacity as variation in executive attention and control. In: Conway, A.R.A., Jarrold, C., Kane, M.J., Miyake, A., Towse, J.N. (eds.) Variation in Working Memory, pp. 21–48. Oxford University Press, New York (2007)
11. King, A.: Discourse patterns for mediating peer learning. In: Cognitive Perspectives on Peer Learning, pp. 87–115. Routledge, London (1999)
12. Kramer, J.: Is abstraction the key to computing? Commun. ACM **50**(4), 36–42 (2007)
13. Kyllonen, P.C., Christal, R.E.: Reasoning ability is (little more than) working-memory capacity. Intelligence **14**(4), 389–433 (1990)
14. Logan, G.D.: Executive control of thought and action. Acta Psychologica **60**(2–3), 193–210 (1985)
15. Manktelow, K., Fairley, N.: Superordinate principles in reasoning with causal and deontic conditionals. Think. Reason. **6**(1), 41–65 (2000)
16. Martini, M., Pinggera, J., Neurauter, M., Sachse, P., Furtner, M.R., Weber, B.: The impact of working memory and the process of process modelling on model quality: investigating experienced versus inexperienced modellers. Scientific Reports 6, 25561, May 2016
17. Meltzer, L. (ed.): Executive Function in Education. The Guilford Press, New York (2007)
18. Miyake, A., Friedman, N., Emerson, M., Witzki, A., Howerter, A., Wager, T.: The unity and diversity of executive functions and their contributions to complex frontal lobe tasks: a latent variable analysis. Cogn. Psychol. **41**(1), 49–100 (2000)
19. Piaget, J.: Zes Psychologische Studies. Van Loghum Slaterus (1969)
20. Pinggera, J., Zugal, S., Weidlich, M., Fahland, D., Weber, B., Mendling, J., Reijers, H.A.: Tracing the process of process modeling with modeling phase diagrams. In: Daniel, F., Barkaoui, K., Dustdar, S. (eds.) BPM 2011. LNBIP, vol. 99, pp. 370–382. Springer, Heidelberg (2012). doi:10.1007/978-3-642-28108-2_36
21. Rasmussen, J.: The abstraction hierarchy. In: Information Processing and Human-Machine Interaction: An Approach to Cognitive Engineering, pp. 13–24. North-Holland (1986)
22. Ribes-Iñesta, E.: Behavior is abstraction, not ostension: conceptual and historical remarks on the nature of psychology. Behav. Philos. **32**(1), 55–68 (2004)
23. Ross, D., Goodenough, J., Irvine, C.A.: Software engineering: process, principles, and goals. Computer **8**(5), 17–27 (1975)
24. Sedera, W., Rosemann, M., Gable, G.: Measuring process modelling success. In: Proceedings of ECIS 2002 (2002)
25. Sins, P.H.M., Savelsbergh, E.R., van Joolingen, W.R.: The difficult process of scientific modelling: an analysis of novices' reasoning during computer based modelling. Int. J. Sci. Educ. **27**(14), 1695–1721 (2005)

26. Waltz, J.A., Knowlton, B.J., Holyoak, K.J., Boone, K.B., Back-Madruga, C., McPherson, S., Masterman, D., Chow, T., Cummings, J.L., Miller, B.L.: Relational integration and executive function in Alzheimer's disease. Neuropsychology **18**(2), 296 (2004)
27. Wilmont, I., Hengeveld, S., Barendsen, E., Hoppenbrouwers, S.: Cognitive mechanisms of conceptual modelling. In: Ng, W., Storey, V.C., Trujillo, J.C. (eds.) ER 2013. LNCS, vol. 8217, pp. 74–87. Springer, Heidelberg (2013). doi:10.1007/978-3-642-41924-9_7

Cognitive Style and Business Process Model Understanding

Oktay Turetken[1]([✉]), Irene Vanderfeesten[1], and Jan Claes[2]

[1] Eindhoven University of Technology, Eindhoven, The Netherlands
{o.turetken,i.t.p.vanderfeesten}@tue.nl
[2] Ghent University, Ghent, Belgium
jan.claes@ugent.be

Abstract. Several factors influence the level of business process model understanding. In this paper, we investigate two personal factors that potentially relate to this level: a reader's cognitive style and theoretical knowledge on business process (BP) modeling. An experiment with 183 graduate students was conducted to explore their differences in cognitive styles using Cognitive Style Index (CSI) and how these relate to their scores in process model understandability. We used two real-life BPMN collaboration diagrams as our process models in our experiment. The results indicate a significant difference between intuitive and analytic students with respect to the level of BP model understandability. The relation between students' theoretical BP modeling and notation competency, and their level of model understanding is also found significant.

Keywords: Business process modeling · Process model comprehension · Model understandability · Cognitive style · Cognitive style index (CSI) · Theoretical business process modeling knowledge

1 Introduction

Business process models are widely used as a means to communicate about the course of actions in a business process among various stakeholders (e.g. process owners, process participants, managers, auditors). They facilitate business process analysis and redesign. Often their construction is a manual effort, e.g. a team of humans map the process, read and interpret the process model, and analyze the process's bottlenecks. Because human interpretation is error-prone, cognitive aspects are important in the manual development of business process models.

Over the past decade many researchers have focused on various challenges that the stakeholders face when conducting business process analysis and (re)design. The structural model characteristics that influence the occurrence of modeling errors and of process model comprehension are extensively researched, e.g. [1–3]. More recently, research efforts have focused on investigating how process modelers create a process model [4, 5], on improving notations and visualizations of process models for better understandability [6–9], on identifying the cognitive biases that may lead to issues in the business process

© Springer International Publishing AG 2017
A. Metzger and A. Persson (Eds.): CAiSE 2017 Workshops, LNBIP 286, pp. 72–84, 2017.
DOI: 10.1007/978-3-319-60048-2_7

management lifecycle [10], and on personal factors of the modelers and model readers that may affect the comprehension of business process models [11, 12].

In this paper, we aim to contribute to the domain of cognitive aspects in business process management by exploring the relation of two personal factors, i.e. the model reader's cognitive style and level of theoretical knowledge on business process (BP) modeling, with process model understanding. This is done empirically with the data from an experiment performed with 183 graduate students. The results show a significant relation of cognitive style and theoretical BP modeling knowledge with process model understanding.

This paper is structured as follows: In Sect. 2 the background on research into process model understandability and cognitive styles is discussed. Section 3 presents the research design including the hypotheses that were tested, and the set-up of the experiment. Finally, results are discussed in Sect. 4, and the paper ends with concluding remarks and outlook in Sect. 5.

2   Background

This section summarizes relevant works on the cognitive aspects of business process modeling and outlines the theory on cognitive styles used for the experiment.

2.1   Related Work

To correctly convey the information that is captured in a BP model to the model reader, the understandability of the model is an important factor researched by many studies, e.g. [1, 3, 13]. Most of these works focus on the structural characteristics of the process model, such as the size, density, and complexity, that influence the readability, syntactic and semantic quality, and the understandability of the model. The main motivation behind this is based on the *cognitive load theory* [14], which states that the more complex a model is, the higher the mental load is to comprehend it. When the mental load is too high, the working memory is overloaded and people tend to make more mistakes [20]. Apart from structural characteristics of the process, literature also suggests a number of personal factors that may influence model understandability such as expertise [1, 12] or cognitive abilities and learning style [11].

From the perspective of creating BP models, some works focus on investigating the way a process modeler creates a process model and link the implemented modeling approach to the syntactic and semantic quality and the understandability of the resulting model (e.g., [4, 15]). One of the main conclusions from these works is that modelers have various styles of modeling and that a structured approach (i.e. chunking the big task of creating the process model into smaller pieces) is a better strategy leading to better process models [16]. It is also concluded that modelers with different profiles may use different modeling strategies to be successful [17]. The authors in [18] present an experiment performed with the objective to understand the factors influencing model readers' preference for the process model representation forms (unstructured, semi-formal or diagrammatic). The results indicate that the preferences for the representation forms vary dependent on application purpose and *cognitive styles* of the participants.

2.2   Cognitive Styles

In the domain of cognitive psychology, the term cognitive style is used to describe the way individual thinks, perceives and remembers information [19]. The Cognitive Style Index (CSI) is one of the ways to measure cognitive style [19]. It is a psychometric measure designed to be used primarily with managerial and professional groups, but has also been applied successfully with students and non-managerial employees [20]. Despite criticisms, CSI is one of the most widely used measures of cognitive style in academic research in the fields of management and education [21–24]. Its construct validity has been indicated in most previous studies through significant correlations with, for example, various personality dimensions and job level [19, 20], and with scores on the Myers–Briggs Type Indicator [25].

As discussed in [20], CSI builds on Ornstein's left-brain/right-brain theory. Ornstein [26] differentiates between analytic and holistic thinking. The former implies processing information in an ordered, linear sequence, whereas the later involves viewing the whole situation at once in order to facilitate the synthesis of all available information. CSI labels these modes of cognition as 'analytic' and 'intuitive' respectively. Figure 1 depicts the intuition-analysis dimension assessed by the CSI. Pure cases of 'intuition' and 'analysis' are located at the two sides. The full exercise of either precludes the adoption of the other. The cognitive style of most people, however, involves elements of both cognitive modes. In the middle range, the 'adaptive' implies a balanced blend of the two modes. Either side of this are the 'quasi-intuitive' and 'quasi-analytical' styles, each of which denotes a tendency towards, but not the full adoption of, one of the extreme cognitive modes. Intuitives are characterized as active, cautious, and impulsive; while analytics as passive, risk taking, and reflective [20].

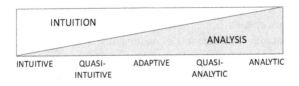

Fig. 1. Continuum of cognitive style [20].

Several researchers have investigated the relationship between CSI and various traits and areas of organizational life, such as job level, occupation, culture, entrepreneurship, personality, etc. Literature suggests that occupations that are likely to favour relatively unconstrained thinking (e.g., creative artists, entrepreneurs) tend to score towards the intuitive end of the CSI scale, whereas those likely to adopt a more structured, systematic approach (e.g., engineers, accountants) tend towards the analytical pole [20]. Similarly, the studies by Brigham et al. [27] and Allinson et al. [28] found that the owner-managers of high growth firms were significantly more intuitive than managers in the general population. This is consistent with the idea that intuition is a necessary quality for those operating in an environment characterised by incomplete information, time pressure, ambiguity and uncertainty. Literature has also studied the relation between CSI and academic performance, and suggests that analytic thinkers are likely to score more highly than their intuitive colleagues - regardless of the subject taught [29, 30].

3   Research Design

Aligned with our research objective, we identified two *independent* variables for the research design: *cognitive style* and *theoretical BP modeling competency*, which are hypothesized to relate to the *understandability task effectiveness*, as a dependent variable representing the level of BP model understanding. Figure 2 presents the research model that we propose. The model suggests that the understanding of a business process model is influenced by its reader's cognitive style and level of theoretical BP modeling competency. Accordingly, we can draw the following hypotheses:

- *H1*. The understandability of a business process model is influenced by model reader's cognitive style.
- *H2*. The understandability of a business process model is positively correlated with the model reader's level of theoretical BP modeling competency.

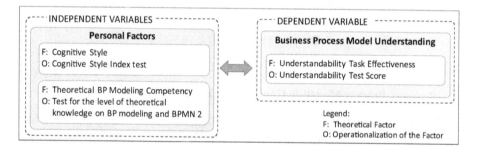

Fig. 2. Research model.

To test these hypotheses, we performed an experiment with the participation of 183 graduate students of the Eindhoven University of Technology, The Netherlands. The experiment was conducted through an extensive questionnaire in 4 main parts. In the first part, the participants went through the CSI test to categorize their cognitive style. The second part was the BP Modeling Competency Test, to assess participants' level of theoretical knowledge on process modeling and BPMN 2.0. As discussed in Sect. 3.2, the test is developed based on the questions in [12]. The last two parts of the questionnaire were designed to measure participants' level of model understanding for *two different process models*. In these parts, the participants were expected to answer 9 understandability questions related to each of these models.

The experiment took place in January 2017 in a single-session and single-location setting. The questionnaire for the experiment was provided through an online web environment. The process models were embedded in the questionnaire environment in such a way that the question and model were presented on the same page (with zoom-in/-out functionalities for the process model). In the subsections that follow, we explain in more detail the design of the experiment, measured variables and their operationalization, as well as the participants of the experiment.

3.1 Cognitive Style Index

We used the Cognitive Style Index (CSI) of Allinson and Hayes [19] as an instrument to measure the intuitive-analytic dimension of cognitive style. The CSI [20] is a 38-item self-report questionnaire. Each item has 'true', 'uncertain' and 'false' response options, and scores of 2, 1 or 0 are assigned to each response with the direction of scoring depending on the polarity of the item [20]. The nearer the total score to the theoretical maximum of 76, the more 'analytical' the respondent, and the nearer to the theoretical minimum of zero, the more 'intuitive' the respondent (see Table 1).

Table 1. CSI score ranges for the five cognitive styles [20].

Style	Score range
Intuitive	0–28
Quasi-Intuitive	29–38
Adaptive	39–45
Quasi-Analytic	46–52
Analytic	53–76

3.2 Business Process Modeling Competency(BPMC) Test

To investigate participants' level of theoretical knowledge on business process modeling and notation, we constructed the Business Process Modeling Competency Test. Taking the questions used in [12] as the basis and extending them, we developed 15 questions related to common process modeling practices (e.g., how basic gateways work, how loops can be defined, etc.) and to the basic constructs of BPMN 2.0. Participants were expected to answer each question by selecting one of the three options: 'yes', 'no', or 'I don't know'. Their competency was measured as the total of correctly answered questions and categorized into 6 groups with the following scheme: level 0 with 0 or 1 correct answers, level 1: 2 to 4, level 2: 5 to 7, level 3: 8 to 10, level 4: 11 to 13, and finally level 5 with 14 to 15 correct answers. Figure 3 shows two examples of questions from the test.

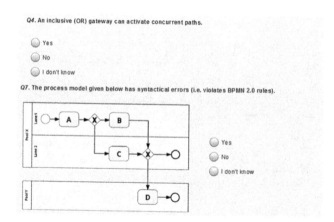

Fig. 3. Example questions from the test on theoretical knowledge on BP modeling and BPMN. (*the complete set of questions is available at:* http://goo.gl/77YAxn).

3.3 Process Models Used for the Experiment

The process models that were used originated from real-life processes that were taking place in a large corporation headquartered in The Netherlands (which employs more than 115,000 employees and operates in over 100 countries worldwide). Among several processes in the company's quality management system, two processes of similar size and nature were selected taking into account their criticality in the business domain in which the company operates. The processes can be considered as large and rich in terms of the interaction taking place between different departments/divisions of the company (each process model incorporates 47 and 46 activity nodes, respectively, and 5 pools).

The selected processes were modelled in BPMN 2.0 based on existing process documentation, and on interviews with process owners and participants. The resulting models were BPMN collaboration diagrams, where the interaction between process participants was explicitly modeled using message flows. The models were subsequently reviewed by modeling experts for syntactical correctness, and validated for their correctness by the domain experts in the company.

These models are already used in our previous works to investigate also other factors of process model comprehension [13]. Accordingly, each process model was re-structured into two other forms, leading to *three forms of representation* for each process model. The first form is the fully-flattened one that shows a process model with all details at once (without the use of groups or sub-processes in BPMN 2.0). The second form makes use of the 'group' construct of BPMN that informally clusters a logically related set of activities on top of the fully-flattened form (similar to the use of 'expanded sub-processes' in BPMN 2.0). The third form uses collapsed sub-processes of BPMN2.0 to create a one-level hierarchy of process models. A collapsed sub-process hides related parts of the model in the higher-level model, but can be accessed separately whenever the reader is interested in the information it contains. Figure 4 shows an example model of one of the processes (process A) in the second representation form.

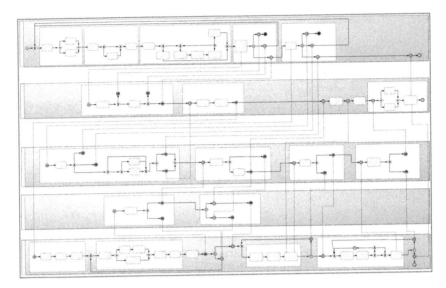

Fig. 4. Process A in *representation 2* (flattened with groups of activities). Note that the model is provided to give an indication of the size and structure of the model, and labels of all process elements are removed. These models were used also in our other experiments [13]. The complete versions of the models with labels are available online at: https://goo.gl/F9oHyg.

3.4   Measuring Process Model Understandability

We used the *understandability task effectiveness* as a metric to quantify the level of understanding that the participants can demonstrate with respect to each process model [1, 31]. Understandability task effectiveness is operationalized by the understandability test score, determined by the number of correctly answered understandability questions for each process model. Accordingly, there was a need to develop a set of representative understandability questions in order to evaluate participants' level of understanding of the processes.

Together with the domain experts in the company, we developed 9 understandability questions for each process. The expert involvement is assumed to assure that each question can be used as a representative and valid way to assess someone's understanding of the processes. Since the quality of these questions has significant influence on the validity of the findings [32], particular attention was paid to develop a set of questions that is balanced in relation to different *process perspectives* (i.e. control flow, resource, and information/data), and different *scopes* (i.e. global and local). A *local* question can be answered by looking only at a single sub-process, while information available in the modularized (high-level) model is sufficient to answer a *global* question. Each question had a multiple-choice design, where respondents were provided with 5 options – the last one always being 'I don't know'. An example question for Process A is as follows:

Qn. If the planned actions for the CAPA are executed, who will receive the Execution Summary Report?	(a) Only CAPA Manager
	(b) Only CAPA Review Board
	(c) Either CAPA Manager or CAPA Review Board
	(d) Both CAPA Manager and CAPA Review Board
	(e) I don't know (unable to tell)

In total, we developed 18 understandability questions (9 for each process model, A and B). Each correctly answered question counts for 1 point for the score, totaling to 18 points max.

3.5   Participants of the Experiment and Blocks

The participants were graduate students of a number of engineering master programs; the majority of which were in operations management (64%), business information systems (14%), and innovation management programs (15%). These students were all enrolled in the same master level course on business process management (BPM), where they participated in the experiment as a final activity taking place few days before the final course examination. During the experiment, each participant was given two process models (A and B) in sequence in a different representation. The participants were randomly assigned to each experiment block.

4   Results

Figure 5 presents the distribution of participants over the cognitive styles and the measured level of knowledge on BP modeling and BPMN 2.0. Accordingly, a high percentage

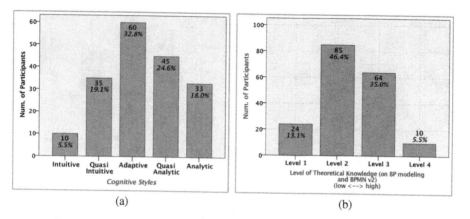

(a)   (b)

Fig. 5. Number of participants with respect to (a) Cognitive Styles (as measured by CSI), and (b) BP modeling Knowledge Level (as measured by BPMC test) (there were no participants at level 0 and level 5, i.e. who correctly answered 0–1, and 14–15 questions, respectively)

of students are adaptive (32.8%), while the number of analytic thinkers (including quasi-) was higher than the intuitive thinkers. This was expected as the participants were students of engineering and/or technology master programs. As for the level of theoretical knowledge on BPM modeling and BPMN 2.0, the majority were at level 2 (46.4%), while only 5.5% were at level 4.

We performed a correlation analysis between the CSI and the level of theoretical knowledge on BP modeling and BPMN 2.0, and found no significant correlation (with a Pearson correlation of -0.077 and $p > 0.29$).

The overall mean score for understandability task effectiveness was 10.1 (out of 18) (st.dev: 2.38). Table 2 presents the descriptive statistics for the variables tested in the experiment. The boxplot diagrams for the understandability task effectiveness over the cognitive styles, and theoretical knowledge level are given in Fig. 6.

Table 2. Descriptive statistics.

Levels	N	Understandability task effectiveness score *(Scale: 0–18)*	
		Mean	St. Dev.
Cognitive Style			
Intuitive	10	7.8	2.4
Quasi Intuitive	35	10.7	2.3
Adaptive	60	9.6	2.4
Quasi Analytic	45	10.2	2.2
Analytic	33	10.7	2.2
Theoretical Knowledge Level			
Level 1	24	9.7	2.2
Level 2	85	9.9	2.2
Level 3	64	10.1	2.7
Level 4	10	12.1	1.8

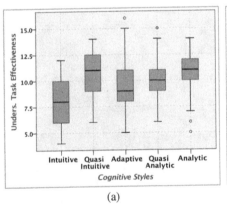

(a)

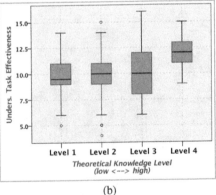

(b)

Fig. 6. Boxplot diagrams for Understandability Task Effectiveness over (a) Cognitive Styles, and (b) Theoretical Knowledge Level (on business process modeling and BPMN 2.0).

In order to identify the appropriate statistical tests that can be used for the testing of our hypotheses, we analyzed the data for conformance with the assumptions of possible statistical tests. The results showed clear deviations from *normality* for the measures of dependent variables over the independent variable (Kolmogorov–Smirnov and Shapiro-Wilk tests of normality, all with p < 0.01). As a result, to evaluate our hypotheses we used a non-parametric test that does not pose assumptions regarding the normality of the data. In particular, we used the Kruskal-Wallis test with stepwise step-down comparisons [33].

4.1 Hypotheses Testing 1: Cognitive Styles

Table 3 shows the results of our tests regarding the hypotheses.

Table 3. Results of the (Kruskal-Wallis) statistical tests.

Independent variables	Understandability task effectiveness	
	H	p
Cognitive style	15.55	*0.004**
Theoretical knowledge level	8.55	*0.036**

We argued in our first hypothesis that the understandability of a BP model is influenced by the model reader's cognitive style. The results of the Kruskal-Wallis test indicate that the effectiveness scores achieved from the understandability questions differ significantly due to the model reader's cognitive style [H(4): 15.55, *p = 0.004*]. According to Kruskal-Wallis *multiple comparison*, the scores attained by *intuitive* thinkers are *significantly lower* than people that possess other cognitive styles. Moreover, the results show that, *analytic* thinkers score *significantly higher* than people with *adaptive* cognitive style. On the other hand, the difference between *quasi-intuitive*, *quasi-analytic* and *adaptive* thinkers is not significant.

The boxplot diagram given in Fig. 6(a) also signifies these effects. We observe a gradual increase in the understandability scores when traversing from intuitive to analytic thinkers, with the exception of *quasi-intuitive* thinkers. Based on the results, we speculate that a model reading task aligns better with analytical skills. In accordance with the cognitive fit theory [34], we can assume that the more a person's intrinsic cognitive style is analytical, the easier model reading task becomes for them, as they may suffer less from cognitive overload. However, we are currently not able to explain why scores from quasi-intuitive thinkers deviate from this linear tendency of increasing understandability as analytic thinking trait begins to dominate.

4.2 Hypotheses Testing 2: Theoretical Knowledge Level

The second hypothesis argues on the positive correlation between the understandability task effectiveness and model reader's level of theoretical knowledge on BP modeling and BPMN 2.0. According to the results presented in Table 3, at least one group of people with a certain level of theoretical knowledge scores significantly different than the other groups (that have different levels of knowledge) [H(3): 8.55, $p = 0.036$].

The results of the Kruskal-Wallis *stepwise multiple comparison* indicate that the understandability scores achieved by people that are characterized as *level 4* (in terms of theoretical knowledge on business modeling and BPMN 2.0) are *significantly higher* than those that are achieved by people that have lower levels of theoretical knowledge. The difference between other levels (1 to 3), on the other hand, are not significant. The boxplot diagram in Fig. 6(b) also gives indication of this result. There is a need to increase the reliability and generalizability of these findings with more respondent data and a better measurement tool (a better version of the BPMC test).

5   Conclusion

In this paper, we found a significant relation of two personal factors (a model reader's cognitive style and theoretical business process (BP) modeling knowledge) to the level of process model understanding. Table 4 summarizes our findings with respect to our hypotheses. The results confirm earlier findings by Mendling et al. [12], which list theoretical BP modeling competency as a significant factor of model comprehension, but add the cognitive profile as an important factor.

Table 4. Summary of hypotheses tests.

Hypothesis	Result	Description
H1. The understandability of a BP model is influenced with model reader's cognitive style	*Supported*	- Intuitive thinkers score significantly lower than people with other cognitive styles
		- Analytic thinkers score significantly higher than adaptive thinkers
		- The difference between quasi-intuitive, quasi-analytic and adaptive thinkers is not significant
H2. The understandability of a BP model is positively correlated with model reader's level of theoretical BP modeling competency	*Supported*	- Participants with high theoretical knowledge (on business modeling and BPMN 2.0) score significantly higher than others with lower theoretical knowledge level

The results from this exploratory experiment may help model readers to understand how they can develop themselves and may play a role in BPM team composition. Furthermore, the insights gained may also advance modeling tools and model representation environments. For example, because people with different characteristics show different levels of model understanding, one may consider to adapt model representations, modeling languages, modeling editors, modeling training, etc. to the different profiles of modelers or model readers.

For future work, we plan to refine current results by collecting more data, we plan to investigate the relation of other personal factors and cognitive profile measurements (such as learning style, field (in)dependency) with the level of process model understanding and we plan to investigate any moderating or confounding personal factors that potentially impact process model understanding.

References

1. Reijers, H.A., Mendling, J.: A study into the factors that influence the understandability of business process models. IEEE Trans. Syst. Man. Cybern. **41**, 449–462 (2011)
2. Mendling, J.: Metrics for Process Models: Empirical Foundations of Verification, Error Prediction and Guidelines for Correctness. Springer, New York (2008)
3. Figl, K.: Comprehension of procedural visual business process models. Bus. Inf. Syst. Eng. **59**, 1–27 (2017)
4. Pinggera, J., Zugal, S., Weidlich, M., Fahland, D., Weber, B., Mendling, J., Reijers, H.A.: Tracing the process of process modeling with modeling phase diagrams. In: Daniel, F., Barkaoui, K., Dustdar, S. (eds.) BPM 2011. LNBIP, vol. 99, pp. 370–382. Springer, Heidelberg (2012). doi:10.1007/978-3-642-28108-2_36
5. Claes, J., Vanderfeesten, I., Reijers, H.A., Pinggera, J., Weidlich, M., Zugal, S., Fahland, D., Weber, B., Mendling, J., Poels, G.: Tying process model quality to the modeling process: the impact of structuring, movement, and speed. In: Barros, A., Gal, A., Kindler, E. (eds.) BPM 2012. LNCS, vol. 7481, pp. 33–48. Springer, Heidelberg (2012). doi: 10.1007/978-3-642-32885-5_3
6. Poppe, E., Brown, R., Recker, J., Johnson, D., Vanderfeesten, I.: Design and evaluation of virtual environments mechanisms to support remote collaboration on complex process diagrams. Inf. Syst. **66**, 59–81 (2017)
7. Mendling, J., Reijers, H.A., Recker, J.: Activity labeling in process modeling: empirical insights and recommendations. Inf. Syst. **35**, 467–482 (2010)
8. Aysolmaz, B., Reijers, H.A.: Towards an integrated framework for invigorating process models: a research agenda. In: BPM Workshops 2014, pp. 11–16 (2014)
9. Aysolmaz, B., Brown, R., Bruza, P., Reijers, H.A.: A 3D visualization approach for process training in office environments. In: Debruyne, C., et al. (eds.) OTM 2016, vol 10033, pp. 436–445. Springer, Cham (2016)
10. Razavian, M., Turetken, O., Vanderfeesten, I.: When cognitive biases lead to business process management issues. In: Dumas, M., Fantinato, M. (eds.) Business Process Management, BPM 2016. LNBIP, vol. 281, pp. 147–156. Springer, Cham (2017). doi: 10.1007/978-3-319-58457-7_11
11. Recker, J., Reijers, H.A., van de Wouw, S.G.: Process model comprehension: the effects of cognitive abilities, learning style, and strategy. Commun. Assoc. Inf. Syst. **34**, 199–222 (2014)
12. Mendling, J., Strembeck, M., Recker, J.: Factors of process model comprehension—Findings from a series of experiments. Decis. Support Syst. **53**, 195–206 (2012)
13. Turetken, O., Rompen, T., Vanderfeesten, I., Dikici, A., Moll, J.: The effect of modularity representation and presentation medium on the understandability of business process models in BPMN. In: La Rosa, M., Loos, P., Pastor, O. (eds.) BPM 2016. LNCS, vol. 9850, pp. 289–307. Springer, Cham (2016). doi:10.1007/978-3-319-45348-4_17
14. Paas, F., Tuovinen, J., Tabbers, H.: Cognitive load measurement as a means to advance cognitive load theory. Educational **38**, 63–71 (2003)
15. Claes, J., Vanderfeesten, I., Pinggera, J., Reijers, H.A., Weber, B., Poels, G.: A visual analysis of the process of process modeling. Inf. Syst. E-bus. Manag. **13**, 1–44 (2014)

16. Claes, J., Vanderfeesten, I., Gailly, F., Grefen, P., Poels, G.: The Structured Process Modeling Theory (SPMT) - A cognitive view on why and how modelers benefit from structuring the process of process modeling. Inf. Syst. Front. **17**, 1401–1425 (2015)
17. Claes, J.: The Structured Process Modeling Method (SPMM) - What is the best way for me to construct a process model? Decis. Support Syst. (2017, in press). doi:10.1016/j.dss.2017.02.004
18. Figl, K., Recker, J.: Exploring cognitive style and task-specific preferences for process representations. Requir. Eng. **21**, 63–85 (2016)
19. Allinson, C., Hayes, J.: The cognitive style index: a measure of intuition-analysis for organizational research. J. Manag. Stud. **33**, 119–135 (1996)
20. Allinson, C., Hayes, J.: The Cognitive Style Index: Technical Manual and User Guide. Pearson Education Ltd, London (2012)
21. Cools, E., Armstrong, S.J., Verbrigghe, J.: Methodological practices in cognitive style research: Insights and recommendations from the field of business and psychology. Eur. J. Work Organ. Psychol. **23**, 627–641 (2014)
22. Armstrong, S.: The influence of individual cognitive style on performance in management education. Educ. Psychol. **20**(3), 323–339 (2000)
23. Armstrong, S., Hird, A.: Cognitive style and entrepreneurial drive of new and mature business owner-managers. J. Bus. Psychol. **24**(4), 419–430 (2009)
24. Hayes, J., Allinson, C.W., Armstrong, S.J.: Intuition, women managers and gendered stereotypes. Pers. Rev. **33**(4), 403–417 (2004). doi:10.1108/00483480410539489
25. Myers, I.B., Briggs, K.C.: The Myers-Briggs Type Indicator. Educational Testing Service, Princeton (1962)
26. Ornstein, R.E.: The Psychology of Consciousness. Harcourt Brace Jovanovich, New York (1977)
27. Brigham, K.H., Sorenson, R.: Cognitive style differences of novice serial and portfolio entrepreneurs: a two-sample test. In: (BCERC-2008) Frontiers of Entrepreneurship Research 2008 (2008)
28. Allinson, C.W., Chell, E., Hayes, J.: Intuition and entrepreneurial behaviour. Eur. J. Work Organ. Psychol. **9**, 31–43 (2000)
29. Backhaus, K., Liff, J.P.: Cognitive styles and approaches to studying in management education. J. Manag. Educ. **31**, 445–466 (2007)
30. Ma, W.W.K., Sun, K., Ma, J.: The influence of cognitive learning styles on the use of online learning environments. In: Cheung, S.K.S., Fong, J., Kwok, L.-F., Li, K., Kwan, R. (eds.) ICHL 2012. LNCS, vol. 7411, pp. 221–230. Springer, Heidelberg (2012). doi:10.1007/978-3-642-32018-7_21
31. Houy, C., Fettke, P., Loos, P.: Understanding understandability of conceptual models – what are we actually talking about? In: Atzeni, P., Cheung, D., Ram, S. (eds.) ER 2012. LNCS, vol. 7532, pp. 64–77. Springer, Heidelberg (2012)
32. Laue, R., Gadatsch, A.: Measuring the understandability of business process models - are we asking the right questions? In: Muehlen, M., Su, J. (eds.) BPM 2010. LNBIP, vol. 66, pp. 37–48. Springer, Heidelberg (2011). doi:10.1007/978-3-642-20511-8_4
33. Field, A.: Discovering Statistics using IBM SPSS Statistics, 4th edn. SAGE Publications Ltd. (2013)
34. Vessey, I., Galletta, D.: Cognitive fit: an empirical study of information acquisition. Inf. Syst. Res. **2**, 63–84 (1991)

Towards a Multi-parametric Visualisation Approach for Business Process Analytics

Stefan Bachhofner$^{(\boxtimes)}$, Isabella Kis, Claudio Di Ciccio, and Jan Mendling

Vienna University of Economics and Business, Vienna, Austria
s.bachhofner@me.com, isabella.kis93@gmail.com,
{claudio.di.ciccio,jan.mendling}@wu.ac.at

Abstract. Visualisation is an integral part of many scientific areas and is reportedly an important tool for learning and teaching. One reason for this is the picture superior effect. Nevertheless, little research endeavour has been carried out so far to effectively apply visualisation principles to the emerging field of business process analytics. In this paper a novel multi-parametric visualisation approach is proposed in such a context. General visualisation principles are used to create, evaluate, and improve the approach in the design process. They are drawn from a wide range of fields, and are synthesised from theory and empirical evidence.

Keywords: Visualisation · Business process analytics · Business process management · Process mining

1 Introduction

Visualisation is a powerful tool for understanding data. In statistics an exploratory data analysis is performed before any statistical method is applied. Any data science process includes a step where the data is explored visually. Medicine and cartography pay particular attention to the colour scheme too. However, in the context of Business Process Management (BPM), little has been done in research to develop visualisation frameworks that effectively help domain experts and process analysts understand the performance of the examined processes. A missed opportunity because information represented visually is more likely to be remembered due to the picture superior effect [7,11]. Business Process Management Systems (BPMSs) play an important role for process-aware organizations. However, BPMS fall short on powerful process analysis tools, especially from the perspective of visualisation. At times, pie charts are used instead of representations that convey the information more accurately.

In this position paper, the importance of powerful visualisation tools in process science is emphasised. In particular, a set of general visualisation principles is presented. Thereupon, we design an unprecedented multi-parametric approach that visually depicts process execution dynamics on a process model, with the representation of multiple performance metrics at once. The presented

© Springer International Publishing AG 2017
A. Metzger and A. Persson (Eds.): CAiSE 2017 Workshops, LNBIP 286, pp. 85–91, 2017.
DOI: 10.1007/978-3-319-60048-2_8

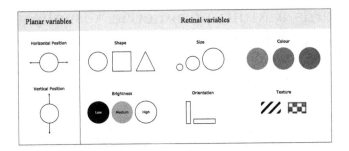

Fig. 1. Visual variables [12]

(a) Rainbow map   (b) Grey map

Fig. 2. Colour perceptual ordering [4] (Color figure online)

framework is based upon the results of a research project held in collaboration with PHACTUM Softwareentwicklung GmbH.

The remainder of the paper is organised as follows. Section 2 introduces the preliminaries from BPM and visualisation. Section 3 proposes our novel multi-parametric visualisation approach for process analytics. Section 4 concludes the paper and outlines further research.

2   Background

BPM is the art and science of overseeing how work is performed in an organisation to ensure consistent outcomes and to take advantage of improvement opportunities [5]. To that extent, the Internet of Events (IoE) [1] opens up new opportunities to process analysts who can rely on the efficient treatment of big data and various sources. Such opportunities include the automated processing of data by means of machine learning techniques and statistical methods, which benefit from the availability of large data sets.

Visualisation is graphical representation of data or concepts [17]. Atomic building blocks of this representation are visual variables, as first described by Bertin et al. [3] and successively clarified by Moody [12] (Fig. 1). Together they form the set of possible visual combinations, i.e., the design space [12]. The chosen visual variable has to preserve the structure of the underlying data [15]. For example, assume a categorical ordinal variable is given such as quantiles or age categories, e.g. young, middle-aged and elderly. In both cases the categories imply an order that has to be maintained. Therefore, a visual variable has to be chosen were perceptual ordering is possible, as shown in Fig. 2. For example, the grey colour map is perceptually ordered because it only varies in brightness (Fig. 2(b)). In contrast, the widely used rainbow colour map is not perceptually ordered because no intuitive sorting of colours is usually sensed by readers (Fig. 2(a)). Another important principle is contextualisation, namely the context+focus paradigm [9, 18], which applies when one wants to focus on a part of a system while showing the context of the system as a whole.

Process mining tools such as Minit [14] and ProM [2][1] use visualisation extensively to display values related to activities' performance metrics such as the frequency with which tasks are carried out – see e.g. the inductive visual miner of ProM [10]. Recently also BPMSs such as Camunda [2] have begun to show measured metrics on process models. However, little has been done in research and practice to visualise more than one performance metric. Visualising two or more metrics at once can prove beneficial because the user can identify patterns and relationships, as it happens with mosaic plots, a multivariate visualisation for categorical data in statistics [16]. The following section clarifies this assumption with a use-case example.

3   Outline of the Approach

To illustrate our approach a student loan application process extracted from [5] is used (Fig. 3). We assume that the process has been completed 100,000 times. The process starts when a loan application is received. First, the application is registered and then the applicants credit-worthiness is checked. Then, the application is either conditionally approved or approved. "Conditionally approve student loan" has been completed 80,000 times and "Approve student loan" 20,000 times, respectively. Finally, the complex activity "Sign loan" is activated and the process is completed. The box plot of the simulated activity durations in days are reported in Fig. 4.

In our approach, the first step is to identify variables that are of interest for the analysis purpose. In this example, we consider *(i)* the number of times they were executed, namely their frequency, and *(ii)* the time the activities need to complete. In addition, we want to show outliers with respect to time, to point out where exceptionally long- or short-lasting tasks took place in relation to the others. To detect the outliers, we classify the registered absolute time values into N categories for every activity, based upon the corresponding quantiles. In the following, we will refer to these categories as c_i where $c_i \in \{c_1, \ldots, c_N\}$. c_i is the category of values between the $(i-1)$-th and the i-th quantile. c_1 and c_N refer to the outliers. In our example, we consider $N = 6$.

As previously stated, maintaining the consistency between the underlying structure of data and the visual representation is essential. In our example, both duration quantiles and frequency are data for which a total order exists. To depict their values, we therefore choose two visual variables which allow for a

---

[1] www.minitlabs.com, www.promtools.org.

[2] https://docs.camunda.org/manual/7.6/webapps/cockpit/bpmn/
process-history-views/#heatmap.

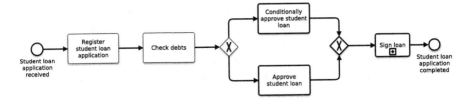

Fig. 3. Example of a student loan application in BPMN [5]

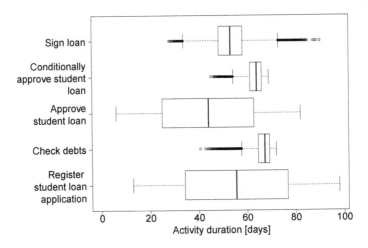

Fig. 4. Box plot of the simulated activity durations

perceptual ordering: The grey colour map to encode quantiles and the size to encode frequency. A third visual variable is implicitly considered because the information is displayed on the process model, hence the additional parameter is the activity for which the metrics are measured. In our example a radial representation of data overlaps the activity boxes of the model to that extent.

Table 1 lists the colour codes assigned to c_i. In the following, we provide an example of how the described categories c_i can be visually translated into the diameter of circles over activities, taking into account the execution frequency. Since the information is displayed on top of a process model, the maximum allowed diameter for each category has to be pre-calculated on the basis of the box size for the activity label containers, due to clear readability reasons. We name such a parameter as $\bar{d}$. For example, assume that the maximum allowed diameter is equal to 180 units[3]. The chosen maximum diameter d for an activity should not overcome the activity box. We recall that the diameter of circles here represents the frequency of executed activities. Therefore we scale it by the maximum frequency among all the activities in the process (in this example, 100,000). For activ-

---

[3] By "unit" we mean any display or printing unit of measurement, such as pixels, centimetres, and the like.

Table 1. Colour codes for categories c_i

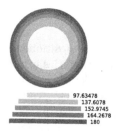

Category	Colour
Outlier below the 1st quantile (c_1)	
Between 1st and 2nd quantile (c_2)	
Between 2nd and 3rd quantile (c_3)	
Between 3rd and 4th quantile (c_4)	
Between 4th and 5th quantile (c_5)	
Outlier above the 5th quantile (c_6)	

Fig. 5. Visual representation of frequency and duration for activity "Check debts"

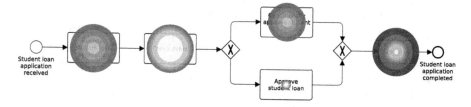

Fig. 6. Multi-parametric visualisation of activities duration and execution frequency

ity "Approve student loan", e.g., we have that $d = \frac{20000}{100000} \cdot \bar{d} = 0.2 * 180 = 36$ units. For "Check debts" $d = 1.0 * 180 = 180$ units instead. The following equation is then used to determine the diameter d_{c_i} of every category c_i.

$$d_{c_i} = \frac{\lambda_i - a}{b - a} \cdot d \tag{1}$$

where λ_i is the upper bound of category c_i, i.e., the i-th quantile, a is the minimum activity duration (i.e., the 0-th quantile), and b is the maximum activity duration (i.e., the 6-th quantile). The formula applied to activity "Check debts", e.g., results in the following diameters:

- $d_{c_2} = \frac{57.66257-40.69231}{71.9848-40.69231} \cdot 180 = 97.63478$
- $d_{c_3} = \frac{64.61496-40.69231}{71.9848-40.69231} \cdot 180 = 137.6078$
- $d_{c_4} = \frac{67.28645-40.69231}{71.9848-40.69231} \cdot 180 = 152.9745$
- $d_{c_5} = \frac{69.24977-40.69231}{71.9848-40.69231} \cdot 180 = 164.2678$

The results are depicted in Fig. 5. Observe that only four diameters were calculated because the diameter for the last category is always equal to d. Repeating this calculations for each activity and projecting the results on the process model leads to the result drawn in Fig. 6. Examining the figure, the outliers can be easily identified by visually extracting the lowest and highest brightened areas. Both activities "Check debts" and "Sign loan" present outliers, but the latter stands out for the ratio of long-lasting executions, as opposed to the former. However, the frequency plays no role in that, as it can be noticed by the correspondence of the diameter of the superimposed circles.

4   Conclusion

This paper has positioned our research endeavour in the visualisation of business process analytics using general visualisation principles based on theory and empirical evidence. In this context, an example has been proposed that deals with the activities' execution times and their frequency simultaneously visualised on a process model. Beyond the proposed example, a multi-parametric visualisation might be improved by considering additional parameters, e.g., a cost matrix depending on actual costs from accounting, or the extent to which a category is considered to be the least favourable to the business purposes. This matrix can then have an influence of the visualisation, e.g., scaling the size of the graphical elements or modifying the colour scheme.

For our future research, we aim at implementing a prototype applying those principles in practice, so as to perform experiments on case studies with researchers and practitioners in the area. Theoretical concepts to compute Process Performance Indicators (PPIs) on the basis of registered process data have been recently proposed in [8]. We will work to integrate the metrics devised in [8] with our approach. Studies on the influence of virtual and augmented reality on visualisation and how BPM can benefit from this new technologies are in our future plans too, also in the light of the recent advancements in the area [6,13].

References

1. van der Aalst, W.M.P.: Data scientist: the engineer of the future. In: Mertins, K., Bénaben, F., Poler, R., Bourrières, J.-P. (eds.) Enterprise Interoperability VI. PIC, vol. 7, pp. 13–26. Springer, Cham (2014). doi:10.1007/978-3-319-04948-9_2
2. van der Aalst, W.M.P., van Dongen, B.F., Günther, C.W., Rozinat, A., Verbeek, E., Weijters, T.: Prom: the process mining toolkit. In: BPM (Demos). CEUR Workshop Proceedings, vol. 489. CEUR-WS.org (2009)
3. Bertin, J.: Semiology of Graphics. University of Wisconsin Press, Madison (1983)
4. Borland, D., Taylor, R.M.: Rainbow color map (still) considered harmful. IEEE Comput. Graph. Appl. **27**, 14–17 (2007)
5. Dumas, M., Rosa, M.L., Mendling, J., Reijers, H.A.: Fundamentals of Business Process Management. Springer Publishing Company, Incorporated (2013)
6. Filonik, D., Rittenbruch, M., Foth, M.: DataChopin - designing interactions for visualisation composition in a co-located, cooperative environment. In: Luo, Y. (ed.) CDVE 2016. LNCS, vol. 9929, pp. 126–133. Springer, Cham (2016). doi:10.1007/978-3-319-46771-9_17
7. Goolkasian, P.: Pictures, words, and sounds: From which format are we best able to reason? J. Gen. Psychol. **127**(4), 439–459 (2000)
8. Kis, I., Bachhofner, S., Di Ciccio, C., Mendling, J.: Towards a data-driven framework for measuring process performance. In: BPMDS (2017)
9. Lamping, J., Rao, R.: The hyperbolic browser: a focus+context technique for visualizing large hierarchies. J. Vis. Lang. Comput. **7**(1), 33–55 (1996)
10. Leemans, S.J.J., Fahland, D., van der Aalst, W.M.P.: Process and deviation exploration with inductive visual miner. In: BPM (Demos), vol. 1295, p. 46 (2014)

11. Lidwell, W., K.H., Butler, J.: Universal principles of Design: A Cross-Disciplinary Reference. Rockport Publishers, Gloucester (2003)
12. Moody, D.: The physics of notations: toward a scientific basis for constructing visual notations in software engineering. IEEE Trans. Softw. Eng. **35**(6), 756–779 (2009)
13. Poppe, E., Brown, R., Recker, J., Johnson, D., Vanderfeesten, I.: Design and evaluation of virtual environments mechanisms to support remote collaboration on complex process diagrams. Inform. Syst. **66**, 59–81 (2017)
14. Puchovsky, M., Di Ciccio, C., Mendling, J.: A case study on the business benefits of automated process discovery. In: SIMPDA, pp. 35–49 (2016)
15. Rogowitz, B.E., Treinish, L.A., Bryson, S.: How not to lie with visualization. Comput. Phys. **10**(3), 268–273 (1996)
16. Theus, M.: Mosaic plots. Wiley Interdisciplinary Reviews: Computational Statistics **4**(2), 191–198 (2012)
17. Tory, M., Möller, T.: Human factors in visualization research. IEEE Trans. Vis. Comput. Graph. **10**(1), 72–84 (2004)
18. Turetken, O., Schuff, D., Sharda, R., Ow, T.T.: Supporting systems analysis and design through fisheye views. Commun. ACM **47**(9), 72–77 (2004)

Investigating the Under-Usage of Code Decomposition and Reuse Among High School Students: The Case of Functions

Ahmad Omar[1(✉)], Irit Hadar[1(✉)], and Uri Leron[2]

[1] Information Systems Department, University of Haifa, Haifa, Israel
ahmadomar3@gmail.com, hadari@is.haifa.ac.il
[2] Faculty of Technology and Science Education, Technion, Haifa, Israel
urileron@gmail.com

Abstract. Functions can provide substantial benefits for programmers. They offer ways that can be used to simplify a given programming task through decomposition, reusability and abstraction. As observed by the first author, a graduate student and high school computer science (CS) teacher, students do not spontaneously use functions when they are asked to solve a certain task; instead they provide one procedural solution, even in situations where functions can clearly be helpful. This research aims to investigate how and when students use functions, as well as the reasons underlying their decisions whether to use them. This paper presents our ongoing research including some results from a pilot study. For data analysis we use the dual-process theory of human cognition and three related concepts: comfort zone, principle of least effort and cognitive laziness. We discuss how these can be useful in order to better understand the problem at hand.

Keywords: Programming · Functions · Reusability · Decomposition · Abstraction dual-process theory · Comfort zone · Principle of least effort · Cognitive laziness

1 Introduction

Decomposition in programming refers to the process of breaking down a higher-level problem into sub-problems, allowing programmers to focus independently on each sub-problem [22]. Functions, procedures and methods are form of abstractions, serving at the same time as decomposition mechanism. They allow dividing a given problem into several simpler tasks, then combining them together for the full solution [19].

Programmers have been observed to under-use different forms of abstractions, thus not fulfilling their potential benefits [11, 12]. In this research, we approach the population of high-school students in the early phases of learning programming, in order to investigate what it is that leads programmers, from the very start of their familiarity and experience with code development, to under-use functions, one of the most basic forms of abstraction. More specifically, the objective of this ongoing research is to investigate how and when students use functions, as well as the reasons underlying their decisions whether to use them. Preliminary results obtained via a pilot study, demonstrate that

© Springer International Publishing AG 2017
A. Metzger and A. Persson (Eds.): CAiSE 2017 Workshops, LNBIP 286, pp. 92–98, 2017.
DOI: 10.1007/978-3-319-60048-2_9

students do not use functions unless they are explicitly instructed to do so, despite their evident familiarity with functions and their proper use. In order to investigate the reasons underlying this behavior, we borrowed a theory and related concepts from cognitive psychology research: the dual-process theory, cognitive laziness, the principle of least effort and, and comfort zone. In this paper we demonstrate how they can useful for making sense of the data obtained.

2   Related Work

Not using functions is not a mistake per-se, but can be inefficient in many cases. It is one of the basic mechanisms for code modularization, decomposition and reusability: "Modularization allows one to decompose a system into functional units, to impose hierarchical ordering on functional usage, to implement data abstractions, and to develop independently useful subsystems" [13]. High modularity allows for separation of concerns, namely dealing separately with each module's details while ignoring other modules' detail, and later with all features of all modules and the relationships between the modules, in order to combine them into a coherent system.

Code modularity facilitates code reuse, namely the ability to use parts of a computer program written previously, aiming to increase productivity and quality in large-scale software development projects [7].

Code modularity mechanisms, such as functions, are forms of abstraction. Abstraction in computer science(CS) involves throwing away detail while keeping the essential structure, and is a skill that is hard to master [1, 14]. Kramer [18] suggests that it is abstraction that differentiates good from weaker students. Functions, in particular, are widely accepted to be a difficult concept to learn [20].

Previous works studying programming skills of high school students have mainly focused on investigating, exploring and reviewing programming mistakes [5, 23]. For example, Brown [5] lists 18 of the most common student mistakes, which vary from simple mistakes, as in the case of incorrect semicolon at the end of a method header, to more complicated ones, such as not controlling the program flow properly. But programming mistakes are not only done by students; even experienced software developers make mistakes, such as confusing inheritance direction or failing to identify objects or classes [11, 12], demonstrating the resilience or such difficulties.

Other directions of research focused on the processes involved in teaching or in learning to program, and on how to improve these processes for better results. Such proposed improvements include, for example, having teachers present real-life examples [3]; letting the students write pseudo-code solutions in order to focus more on the structure and not be held back by syntax [8]; allocating more time in class for exercises, with the teacher as guider [2]; and, letting students learn from their mistakes [10]. No such improvement technique was examined in the specific context of functions.

3   Theoretical Background

The dual-process theory deals with the question of why people make mistakes that could have been avoided given their own knowledge [16]. The theory suggests that two separate cognitive systems operate in our mind: intuitive and analytical thinking. The first system (S1) deals with immediate, automatic thinking processes, based on heuristics. The second system (S2) is responsible for analytical processing. S1 results in fast and automatic solutions, while S2 in slower, consciously analyzed ones [16].

Cognitive laziness refers to the situation in which people may be content with a "good enough" solution, despite their awareness that a better solution can be achieved if they invest more effort [9]. Although there may be a better solution, people tend to choose the solution that is enough for their immediate goals. Intuitive judgment and common sense are examples of mechanism used due to cognitive laziness [21].

The principle of least effort explains that people (or even animals or smart machines) will naturally choose the path of least effort, with the least resistance, having the desire to reach things quickly and easily [25]. Accordingly, a person facing a certain situation, tends to choose the solution with the least effort from all possible solutions rising in the horizon (as perceived by that specific person) [6].

Comfort zone is a situation in which a person behaves in an anxiety neutral condition, and acts limitedly, in order to sustain a steady, risk-free state of tasks' performance [24]. The term comfort zone refers to a psychological state in which a person feels comfortable, at ease and in control [24], and suggests that individuals may choose the less stressful and challenging solution, in order to be in the more comfortable and less adventurous state, from their point of view [4].

4   Pilot Study – Method and Settings

The objectives of this research are to empirically explore our initial observation that students do not use functions when they deal with programming tasks, unless they are explicitly asked to do so, and to understand the reasons underlying this behavior.

The population of pilot study included 10 students of the 12th grade, who majored in CS in the school in which the first author teaches. These students had already learned and exercised the use of functions and were trained in programming tasks.

During the study, the students had free access to their books and notebooks. Each student was handed three worksheets which included programming tasks. The worksheets were given one at a time; the next sheet given only after the participants completed the previous one, in order to prevent them from checking questions in the next worksheet thus possibly affecting the way they solve the questions in the current one.

The first worksheet included three tasks, with a shared functionality to all, but with no further information. It instructed to add a number to all items in a given array, with the tasks differing only in the value of the added number. The second worksheet included three tasks of the same level with a shared functionality and an instruction, at the bottom, asking participants to pay attention to what is common in the tasks. The third worksheet also included three tasks of the same level, with an instruction to write a function for the common functionality and to use it to solve the three tasks.

Data collection was based mainly on: (1) Written solutions collected from the participants after each task; and (2) group interviews [17] about their solutions. We used a semi-structured approach with no rigorous set of questions, so to allow diversion [15].

In analyzing the worksheets' answers, we looked for general solutions, rather than fully correct ones; we did not consider syntax or any other compilation errors but rather considered the intention behind the students' answers. We classified the answers to those using functions and those that do not. During the data analysis, we looked for explanations for the obtained results. Specifically, in analyzing the qualitative data from the transcribed group interview, we mapped students' quotes to a corresponding cognitive concept based on an initial set of guidelines we developed:

Table 1. Preliminary guidelines for mapping explanations and cognitive concepts

Explanation type (self-report)	Mapped to
A student did not use functions because s/he did not feel comfortable enough with it, despite being aware to this possibility	Comfort Zone
A student considered different alternatives including functions, and settled, consciously for a "good enough" solution[a]	Cognitive laziness
A student considered different alternatives, including functions, and chose, consciously, the possibility that was perceived to save effort (cognitive effort, time, writing, etc.)	Principle of least effort
A student wrote the first things that came up to mind, without considering other possibilities	General – dual-process theory

[a]The "good enough" solution is not necessarily the one that requires the least effort; in fact, using functions requires the least effort overall (writing less code). When *cognitive laziness* takes over, it leads to a "good enough" solution considering the least effort in the *short* term (merely for solving the first task).

5   Results

In worksheet1, all students used a *for* loop, for each task, while changing the value of the added number each time. Not even a single student wrote a function for the common functionality for reusing it in the different tasks. When the students were later whether they had noticed a common functionality between the tasks, one student raised his hand. When asked why he did nothing about it, he answered: "I didn't know what to do with this common functionality; I just solved the question as required."

In worksheet2, all students used *for* loops, the same way as in worksheet1, even though they were asked here to pay attention to what is common between the tasks. When asked about their solutions, all students stated that they had noticed the comment about the commonality. When asked why they did not use a function instead of repeating the same code with a change of value, they gave the following explanations:

1. "I wrote the first thing that crossed my mind."

2. "I answered without thinking too much; it was almost automatic."
3. "I answered in the easiest way."
4. "It is more comfortable for me to solve it this way."
5. "The number of questions is small, why the effort?"
6. "I answered in the simplest way, straightforward, without complication."
7. "I answered in the way with the least possibility to make mistakes."
8. "The tasks did not require us to write a function. Had that been a requirement in the assignment, I would have no problem doing that."
9. "There were only few questions and the questions themselves were easy."

In worksheet3, the students were asked explicitly to write a specific function and to use it in solving the set of tasks given in this worksheet. All the students, with no exception, wrote the function properly and used it in solving the three questions.

When they were asked if they had faced any difficulty writing the function or using it, they all answered with a no. When we further asked them why, unlike in the previous two worksheets, in this one they had wrote and used a function for the common functionality, they explained that it was because they were asked to do so.

Trying to make sense of the observation that students do not take advantage of functions and reuse, despite their proven knowledge and capability to do so, we mapped their explanation quotes to the four cognitive psychological concepts according to the guidelines presented in Table 1. The mapping is presented in Table 2.

Table 2. Theory and related quotes

Cognitive theory/concept	Related quotes
Comfort zone	4, 7
Cognitive laziness	6, 8
Principle of least effort	3, 5, 9
Dual processing theory	1, 2

This demonstration of mapping students' explanations to the cognitive concepts presents some promise toward an understanding of the different sources leading to the avoidance of using functions. The next step of the research will involve a higher-volume data collection to allow for a more quantitative investigation and generalization of the results. In addition, since students' explanations do not necessarily accurately reflect their actual thinking processes, we plan to use the think-aloud protocol as a complementary method in the research in order to mitigate this threat.

6   Discussion and Future Work

The pilot study included a small number of participants, all belonging to the same school. The full study will include 12th grade students from four high schools, with the participation of about 30 students from each school. The schools will be of different levels, different teaching languages, and different populations: two private schools and two public ones, with Arabic or Hebrew as teaching languages. These settings are designed so to improve the external validity of the findings.

As a result of this research we hope to expend our understanding on the underlying cognitive processes that lead to the under-usage of functions. Such understanding may lay the foundations for developing means for promoting functions' use, by overcome the identified barriers for using functions. We will also provide a set of guidelines for mapping given behavior to cognitive states possibly triggering this behavior. These guidelines could be used in the context of function usage in programming specifically, or generally when investigating any under-used tool or information that cannot be explained by the investigated individuals' lack of knowledge.

References

1. Aharoni, D., Leron, U.: Abstraction is hard in computer-science too. In: Pehkonen, E. (ed.) Proceedings of the 21st Conference of the International Group for the Psychology of Mathematics Education. University of Helsinki, Lahti, Finland (1997)
2. Black, T.R.: Helping novice programming students succeed. J. Comput. Sci. Coll. **22**(2), 109–114 (2006)
3. Börstler, J., Hall, M.S., Nordström, M., Paterson, J.H., Sanders, K., Schulte, C., Thomas, L.: An evaluation of object oriented example programs in introductory programming textbooks. In: ACM SIGCSE Bulletin, vol. 41(4), pp. 126–143 (2010)
4. Brown, M.: Comfort zone: model or metaphor? J. Outdoor Environ. Educ. **12**(1), 3 (2008)
5. Brown, N. C., Altadmri, A.: Investigating novice programming mistakes: educator beliefs vs. student data. In: Proceedings of the 10th Annual Conference on International Computing Education Research, pp. 43–50. ACM (2014)
6. Collan, M.: Lazy user behavior, MPRA Paper No. 4330 (2007). http://mpra.ub.uni-muenchen.de/4330/
7. da Silva, M.F., Werner, C.L.: Packaging reusable components using patterns and hypermedia. In: Proceedings of 4th International Conference Software Reuse, pp. 146–155. IEEE (1996)
8. Fidge, C., Teague, D.: Losing their marbles: syntax-free programming for assessing problem-solving skills. In: Proceedings of the 11th Australasian Conference on Computing Education, vol. 95, pp. 75–82. Australian Computer Society, Inc. (2009)
9. Fiske, S.T.: Thinking is for doing: portraits of social cognition from daguerreotype to laserphoto. J. Pers. Soc. Psychol. **63**(6), 877 (1992)
10. Ginat, D.: The greedy trap and learning from mistakes. In: ACM SIGCSE Bulletin, vol. 35(1), pp. 11–15 (2003). ACM
11. Hadar, I.: When intuition and logic clash: the case of the object-oriented paradigm. Sci. Comput. Program. **78**(9), 1407–1426 (2013)
12. Hadar, I., Leron, U.: How intuitive is object-oriented design? Commun. ACM **51**(5), 41–46 (2008)
13. Hashim, K., Key, E.: A software maintainability attributes model. Malays. J. Comput. Sci. **9**(2), 92–97 (1996)
14. Hazzan, O., Kramer, J.: Assessing abstraction skills. Commun. ACM **59**(12), 43–45 (2016)
15. Hove, S.E., Anda, B.: Experiences from conducting semi-structured interviews in empirical software engineering research. In: 11th IEEE International Symposium on Software Metrics (2005)
16. Kahneman, D.: Maps of bounded rationality: a perspective on intuitive judgment and choice. Nobel Prize Lecture **8**, 351–401 (2002)

17. Kontio, J., Lehtola, L., Bragge, J.: Using the focus group method in software engineering: obtaining practitioner and user experiences. In: Proceedings of the International Symposium Empirical Software Engineering ISESE 2004, pp. 271–280. IEEE (2004)
18. Kramer, J.: Is abstraction the key to computing? Commun. ACM **50**(4), 36–42 (2007)
19. Meyer, B.: Object-Oriented Software Construction. Prentice Hall, New York (1988)
20. Paz, T., Leron, U.: The slippery road from actions on objects to functions and variables. J. Res. Math. Educ. **40**, 18–39 (2009)
21. Pearl, J.: Heuristics: intelligent search strategies for computer problem solving (1984)
22. Rosson, M.B., Alpert, S.R.: The cognitive consequences of object-oriented design. Hum. Comput. Interac. **5**(4), 345–379 (1990)
23. Sirkiä, T., Sorva, J.: Exploring programming misconceptions: an analysis of student mistakes in visual program simulation exercises. In: Proceedings of the 12th Koli Calling International Conference on Computing Education Research, pp. 19–28. ACM (2012)
24. White, A.: From comfort zone to performance management. White & MacLean Publishing (2009)
25. Zipf, G.K.: Human behavior and the principle of least effort: An introduction to human ecology. Ravenio Books (2016)

T4SIS4T – Teaching for Smart Information Systems – Smart Information

Design Thinking in Multidisciplinary Learning Teams: Insights from Multidisciplinary Teaching Events

Meira Levy[✉]

Department of Industrial Engineering and Management,
Shenkar College of Engineering Design and Art, 12 Anna Frank Street, 52526 Ramat-Gan, Israel
lmeira@shenkar.ac.il

Abstract. The design thinking approach which shapes the design culture of many organizations today, focuses on users' experiences, particularly their emotional ones, and strives to develop smart technologies and other complex systems and make them simple, intuitive and pleasurable. During design thinking processes, development teams are required to build empathy with users, observe their behavior and conclude and describe what they want and need, by using emotional language such as desire, love and aspire. Moreover, emotional attributes and notations are inserted into current modeling languages for expressing emotional goals and motivations for realizing users' perceptions of systems. For fostering design thinking capabilities, universities offer multidisciplinary learning opportunities where engineers and designers learn and practice together design thinking in development processes. In this regard, Shenkar, College of Engineering, Design and Art, provides students with several multidisciplinary learning opportunities in courses and workshops. This paper reports on these opportunities and brings insights and recommendations for enhancing the next multidisciplinary teaching events. The recommendations draw on the current body of literature in the areas of design thinking approach, agile framework and creativity, and address: defining open challenges that appeal to each discipline; handling teams' working process and responsibilities; and outlining expected solution that encompasses multidisciplinary capabilities.

Keywords: Design thinking · Creativity · Multidisciplinary team · Emotions · Agile framework

1 Introduction

In the new global economy era multidisciplinary knowledge and capabilities are required for gaining competitive advantages and foster innovation [1, 2]. Previous research addressed the need to enable effective collaboration among people from different disciplines, and found that successful multidisciplinary encounters depend on tailoring the selection of a theme, participants, and location to the encounter's particular objectives [3]. In particular, universities are revising their curriculum for including disciplines like social science, humanities, cultural and management studies so students will be prepared to the changing needs of industry and society which seek to bridge the gap that exists between producers and consumers of technology. Moreover, students need to understand

© Springer International Publishing AG 2017
A. Metzger and A. Persson (Eds.): CAiSE 2017 Workshops, LNBIP 286, pp. 101–109, 2017.
DOI: 10.1007/978-3-319-60048-2_10

the financial, business, environmental economic and social constraints in which engineers operate [4]. For this aim, multidisciplinary learning opportunities are organized where participants are familiarized with one another's profession and learn to appreciate dissimilar viewpoints [5]. In line with this, innovation can no longer be considered as a 'functional problem' but rather it touches on all aspects of society including cultural and environmental issues [6, 7]. Following that, comes the idea that research and development (R&D) functions are not enough to drive innovation, and novel perspective requires involving the users' experience as part of the R&D processes [7, 8]. Within this new business environment, design skills have a central role in driving innovation processes and bridging different fields as engineering, humanities, social science, economic and production disciplines [9]. These design skills foster design thinking in innovation management, encompassing creative, proactive and empathic approach to connect different bodies of knowledge in order to shape innovative solutions [10, 11] as Meyer [12] phrased:

> "Combining strategic objectives and technical business requirements with emotions and conceptual thinking, design thinking is used to create interactions between people and systems, products or technology, with a goal of making those interactions simple, intuitive, and empathetic." p. 42

Although the literature suggests that multidisciplinary programs are beneficial for broadening the students' perspectives, there are scant reports that describe the interdisciplinary educational experiences and the interactions that occur among their participants. This paper presents an empirical study on several multidisciplinary learning events which include one workshop and two courses and its main contribution is outlining recommendations for leveraging the learning experience of students from all disciplines. The paper is organized as follows: first related background regarding the cognitive capabilities underpinning design and creativity in multidisciplinary teams is presented in Sect. 2. This is continued in Sect. 3 with the presentation of the agile framework [13] as a practitioners' framework that aims at delivering a faster designed outcome in the context of diversity and design thinking. This background served as the theoretical ground for analyzing the empirical study, presented next, followed with the study's analysis and findings, and concludes with recommendations and future research direction.

2   Design and Creativity

The term design evolved from the original meaning of design and production of an object, to two different terms design as art and design as engineering [2].

> "Design is the conscious decision-making process by which information (an idea) is transformed into an outcome, be it tangible (product) or intangible (service)." p. 17

Hence, design requires decision making, based on comparing alternatives, exploring and experimenting which may lead to innovation. Today, there is a growing awareness of the need to create multifunctional teams which include designers and engineers during new product development process, as a strategic tool, for gaining competitive advantage and foster innovation [2, 6]. Combining capabilities of creators, empathizers, pattern recognizers and meaning makers with logical and linear thinkers, can change the way organizations operate [1]. Moreover, designers are educated to deal with fuzzy and unpredictable situations and projects that require personal perspective, visual presentations, emotional involvement and almost no quantification [7]. Conversely, managers and engineers, study accounting, finance, and related analytical subjects.

While the idea of assembling multidisciplinary team in design processes is essential to innovation, people with different professional backgrounds often have different value system that can lead to misunderstanding and conflict [2]. Nevertheless, western society is changing because forces such as globalization, nonmaterial yearnings and powerful technologies are reducing computer-like professions. Therefore, multidisciplinary working practices are required, and a new approach is needed for fostering abilities of empathy, understanding human interactions and eliciting purpose and meaning [1]. The challenge is to enable the integration of sequential, logical and analytical thinking with nonlinear, intuitive, and holistic thinking [1]. Former study pointed at the important role of teammates' background knowledge and experience to foster creativity in multidisciplinary teams. The study also claimed that a good balance between individual performance and team dynamics is vital to the success in a multidisciplinary team process [14].

3   Agile Framework, Diversity and Design Thinking

The agile framework emerged towards the end of the 20th century and is accepted today as one of the main software development management styles in many software companies. Although the agile framework clearly originates in the profession of software development, its novelty is in addressing the human aspects of the process rather than the technological ones and its main guidelines are applicable to various domains beyond software development processes [13]. The agile framework addresses several aspects in teams' work. Among them, the most relevant ones to the multidisciplinary teams presented in this study, are: teams' leadership; teammates' responsibility; iterative development and testing processes; team's goal and time management; transparency and knowledge sharing; and customer involvement.

It is, nowadays, accepted that the transparent nature of agile environments fosters diversity since team members have more opportunity to be exposed to new ideas and perspectives, thus enhancing the chance for innovation. According to Hazzan and Dubinsky [15], agile teams may benefit from this enhanced diversity in several ways. First, the more diverse a team is, the more wide-ranging perspectives are elicited; consequently, teammates are exposed to others' perspectives and can use these different viewpoints in different or new (problem-solving) situations. Second, the project deliverable itself may be improved since the expression of different perspectives with respect to a specific aspect of the deliverable enhances the chances that subtle issues will emerge; consequently, additional factors are considered when decisions related to the said deliverable are made. Third, the entire process is questioned more when diverse opinions are expressed, and, once again, the team may gain a more argument-based process. Fourth, diversity reduces resistance to new ideas and establishes an open atmosphere towards alternative opinions. Finally, as more companies become global, diversity is becoming an integral characteristic of teams and, therefore, cannot be over-looked. It is but natural to assume that a team that welcomes diversity will assimilate its behavior in this global market in a more natural and successful manner.

The design thinking approach puts the customer up-front, similar to the agile approach, however it emphasizes on building empathy with users, observing their behavior and drawing conclusions about what people want and need. In addition, it fosters the use of emotional language, such as desires, aspirations, engagement, and experience, to describe products and users [11].

Lately, the agile and design thinking approaches were integrated to one framework for delivering a faster outcome in an innovative, dynamic environment that addresses the need to rethink the customer needs [16]. In addition, emotional attributes and notations are inserted into current modeling languages for expressing emotional goals and motivations for realizing users' perceptions of systems [17].

4 Empirical Study

4.1 Method and Settings

The research took place at the Israeli Shenkar College of Engineering, Design and Art, which is unique in the extent to which engineering and visual design schools co-exist and collaborate. There are several learning events at Shenkar where students from engineering, design and art participate in multidisciplinary learning events. I will briefly elaborate on the various experiences that served as the research fields in the empirical study:

1. Shenkar's annual 'Jam Week' which brings together lecturers and students from the Engineering, Design and Art schools, in a variety of joint workshops in which multidisciplinary teams brainstorm and create products that combine design, art and technology. I was a co-organizer in one of these workshops, where the study reported here took place, involving 40 students, 19 from the engineering school and 21 from the design and art schools.

2. The 'The Interdisciplinary Lab' course which was given by lecturers from the Software Engineering and Visual Communications departments and an external instructor who specializes in data journalism. The course was offered to third year design students specializing in interaction design and to software engineering students specializing in mobile and web platforms. There were around 50 students in the course, 30 from the engineering school and 20 from the design school.

3. The course 'Smart Interactions Design in the Era of Internet of Things' given in the 'Kadar center for design and technology', in which students from Design, Art and Engineering schools participated and created innovative interaction solutions to challenges given by the lectures who manage the Kadar center. There were 10 students in the class, 7 from the design and art schools and 3 from the engineering school.

While the first event was a four-day workshop, the two others were full semester courses. In all the three learning events the students had to cope with ill-structured problems, which will be presented in the next section.

As a researcher I participated in all these events, during the first event, the annual 'Jam week', as a participant observer and during the two others, as an observer. The main research objective was to learn how multidisciplinary teams work and collaborate. According to this objective the following research questions (RQs) were:

RQ1: Which design processes are practiced in multidisciplinary teams?
RQ2: What disciplines are actually represented in the design process?
RQ3: Do the teams' solutions exhibit the various capabilities of the teammates?

I observed and conducted several unstructured interviews with the students and lecturers from all the events. During the field observations notes were taken, focusing on conversations among the teammates, the guidelines presented by the lectures, the feedback that were given by the students, lecturers, and guests and the processes that took place during the learning events. In addition, students from the various disciplines were interviewed regarding the role they took in their teams and their perceptions about the learning experience. In each event I conducted around 5 interviews in case I had to clarify an observed issue, when students approached me for sharing insights or when I wanted to get their feedbacks. The gathered data were qualitatively analyzed [18]. Using its inductive methodology, the notes taken during the observations and interviews were mapped to the emergent categories of professional discussions; professional tools; solutions' requirements; and students' engagement.

4.2 Analysis and Findings

The analysis of the gathered data showed that students were eager to meet colleagues from various disciplines, for extending their perceptions and learning experience. This was expected, otherwise students would have not participated in these events (only the first event is mandatory). Moreover, the students at Shenkar have lately started a new initiative, entitled "Dots" (aiming at connecting the dots) for fostering multidisciplinary learning events. With regard to the research questions presented above the analysis revealed:

RQ1: During the three learning events, for each challenge's solving process, the teams went through three phases: ideation, implementation and presentation. The terminology used by the lecturers and teams was design rather than engineering oriented. The learning events started with the presentations of challenges in a brief format, which is a common practice in design and art courses, where students get an open question or challenge which lead them to research and brainstorming. For example, in the course "The Interdisciplinary Lab" they got a data file in which they had to find meaningful paths and present it in an infographic design; in the course "Smart Interactions Design" they got a challenge to create users' interaction experience in the open space of Shenkar. In contrary, engineers are used to more defined challenges with detailed requirements in a specific context. Moreover, in the three learning events, during the ideation phase, there was an emphasis not to think about the technology but rather on the users' experience, as if there were no technological barriers. The students got ideation triggers such as "What the users will feel?" "What kind of dialogue it evokes?" "Don't think how to implement the ideas, just brainstorm", "What is the beauty in this idea?"

The shared theme of this year 'Jam week' workshops was "Changing from the bottom, how academy can contribute to its environment?" While it is a very social theme, in many workshops the integration of social design and technical implementation could have been applied. For example, during my workshop which was entitled "From social networks to human networks", they had to solve challenges presented by several social organizations. The students from all disciplines got a guideline to use their professional capabilities, however, all the teams produced physical objects, but only few added technologic suggestions and outcomes, although it could have enhanced their proposed solutions. In one case, a team produced creative toys made of recycled plastics and textiles to kindergarten of foreign workers' children, as shown in Fig. 1. However, they could have added a social software platform around their idea for enabling the creation of a social community for fostering recycling textiles and plastics.

Fig. 1. Toys created in the 'Jam Week' workshop

During the second phase, after each team decided on which idea to focus, the implementation phase started. In the courses that lasted for a whole semester, students could actually build a working prototype, consisting of either a physical object or infographic application, which required software development and in the "Smart Interactions Design in the Era of Internet of Things" course, hardware implementations as well. In this phase, the design and art students were responsible to find the materials or create art works that suit their ideas, and the engineering students dealt mainly with the technical and technological issues.

The third phase of the process was presenting the final products and involved, besides the teams and lecturers, guests who were not part of the learning experience. The guests were either professionals in the different disciplines or the users that initiated the challenges. The feedback often praised the creative ideas and sometimes pointed at difficulties to implement the ideas in real settings

RQ2: During the ideation phase, the design and art students used storyboarding, which is a common visual practice in the design domain, in which designers sketch user experience scenarios; and video prototyping in the "Smart Interactions Design in the Era of Internet of Things" course.

In the all three learning events, multidisciplinary teams could have faced with the need to develop a technological solution, either in the form of software or hardware, in addition to the design challenge. Nevertheless, while visual design practices were employed, especially in the brainstorming and prototyping phases, almost no engineering design practices, such as textual modeling frameworks (e.g., ERD), were used. Although the engineering students were equipped with the necessary design modeling knowledge, they did not use it, and moved directly from high level abstraction of the ideation phase, to the technical implementation phase of their projects. In addition, all the teams' development processes were not managed in professional ways, although there were students who came from the Industrial Engineering and Management department, with knowledge about project management practices. Neither of the teams defined formal management responsibilities (besides professional ones that exhibited design or engineering capabilities), nor used any of the agile practices which were discussed in Sect. 3 above.

RQ3: The final projects exhibited the capabilities of the teammates' to some extent which differed in each learning experience. The design capabilities were manifested in all the projects, dealt very seriously and the designers were very anxious to deliver the outcome in the most professional manner. Moreover, the feedback they got throughout the experience emphasized design and not engineering issues. The technical development should have mainly functioned properly, implementing the design requirements. During the 'Jam week' events, due to the very short time of the experience, only in one challenge the students managed to present a manifestation of their technological solution and actually built a site using the Wix[1] platform, which is a commercial free platform for creating websites. In the other challenges they came with ideas, without bringing it to some sort of professional outcome, neither as models nor prototypes. In the two other courses the technological parts were prototypes that reflected the designers' requirements. The outcomes were missing engineering design models which could have later be developed to more matured products. Moreover, feedback from the presentation phases strengthened the overall impression that if the engineering contributions were professionally manifested throughout the learning event, the prototypes, either built or suggested, could have addressed more real setting considerations and solutions

---

[1] http://www.wix.com/.

From the above it shows that there was no balance in the multidisciplinary teams between design and engineering practices. An engineering student summed this in his words:

"The idea to bring together students from engineering and design is great, and Shenkar is the best place to leverage this up. In order to enhance this experience I suggest to use the managerial practices of Industrial Engineering and Management students who possess managerial capabilities and can use risk and time management tools. When the challenge is presented only with design words, the engineers do not relate to it and do not connect the words to their profession. Therefore, it should be more balanced so everyone can feel connected. In my workshop the process started to advance when an engineer said, we must go on we can't talk all day about the design of one button, it shouldn't be perfect…"

5 Conclusion

The paper reports on an empirical research conducted during multidisciplinary learning events at Shenkar, in which students from the Engineering, Design and Art schools collaboratively worked in multidisciplinary teams. Such experience is important to students before entering the job market, as nowadays companies develop 'smart information systems' through design thinking processes that involve multidisciplinary perspectives and diverse teams [6]. Hence, realizing the way to better teach students during multidisciplinary learning events is vital for preparing them to real jobs' demands.

The study revealed that students were enthused to participate in such experience and found it educational and enjoyable. However, according to the presented study, the learning experience can be leveraged so students, from all disciplines, can utilize these events to their full potential. The data gathered in the various experiences shows that while design perspectives are emphasized and discussed, the engineering and management ones are hardly mentioned and practiced. The outcomes of the multidisciplinary teams show that adding engineering and management practices to the learning processes could have leveraged the teams' work in both their working processes as well as their final products. Modeling the products' with engineering capabilities could have helped considering different users and processes, making the abstract design ideas more realistic and robust that could have applied to additional audiences. In addition, managing the whole process could have made the learning experience relevant to all the teammates who would have been more engaged in the learning events and responsible to their roles. Therefore, in line with previous study [14], the main recommendation is elevating the potential of teammates so each one of them will feel responsible and equally contribute to the final product. There should be a balance between open, free of barriers thinking and more realistic, down to earth solutions, otherwise there will be a gap between the ideation and implementation phases. Following, the terminology used in multidisciplinary learning experiences should be consist of the different disciplines' terminology and appeal to the whole teammates. In addition, employing the agile framework within the multidisciplinary learning experience can contribute to manage the whole process and foster design thinking, as found in related study [16].

This study sheds light on the potential and challenges of multidisciplinary teams in development processes in general and in information system development processes in particular. Nowadays, when universities seek new forms of multidisciplinary learning that foster collaboration, problem solving and innovation [19], this study can help in building programs with well-defined projects that stimulate students to achieve fruitful results. However, the generalization of this preliminary research may be limited as it reports on few experiences in one academic institute. Future research will continue to explore and study multidisciplinary learning experiences in various domains and institutes.

References

1. Pink, D.H.: A Whole New Mind: Why Right-Brainers Will Rule the Future. Riverhead Books, New York (2005)
2. Stamm, V.B.: Managing Innovation, Design and Creativity, 2nd edn. Wiley, Hoboken (2008)
3. Bridle, H., Vrieling, A., Cardillo, M.: Preparing for an interdisciplinary future: a perspective from early-career researchers. Futures 53, 22–32 (2013)
4. Parashar, K.M., Parashar, R.: Innovations and curriculum development for engineering education and research in India. Procedia – Soc. Behav. Sci. 56, 685–690 (2012)
5. Taneli, Y., Yurtkuran, S., Kirli, G.: A multidisciplinary design exercise: Myndos excavation site. Procedia – Soc. Behav. Sci. 106, 120–129 (2013)
6. Rigby, D.K., Gruver, K., Allen, J.: Innovation in turbulent times. Harvard Business Review (2009). http://hbr.org/2009/06/innovation-in-turbulent-times/ar/1. Accessed 6 Mar 2014
7. Chesbrough, H.W.: Open Innovation: The New Imperative for Creating and Profiting from Technology. Harvard Business Press, Boston (2003)
8. Norman, D., Verganti, R.: Incremental and radical innovation: design research versus technology and meaning change. Des. Issues 30(I), 78–96 (2014)
9. Deserti, A., Rizzo, F.: Design and the culture of enterprise. Des. Issue 30, 36–56 (2014)
10. Brown, T.: Strategy by design. Fast Company 95, 3–8 (2005)
11. Kolko, J.: Design thinking comes of age. Harvard Bus. Rev. 93(9), 66–71 (2015)
12. Meyer, L.M.: Design thinking a view through the lens of practice. OD Pract. 47, 4 (2015)
13. Hazzan, O., Dubinsky, Y.: Agile Anywhere - Essays on Agile Projects and Beyond. Springer Briefs in Computer Science. Springer, Heidelberg (2014)
14. D'souza, N., Dastmalchi, M.R.: Creativity on the move: exploring little-c (p) and big-C (p) creative events within a multidisciplinary design team process. Des. Stud. 46, 6–37 (2016)
15. Hazzan, O., Dubinsky, Y.: Agile Software Engineering. UTiCS. Springer, London (2008)
16. Gurusamy, K., Srinivasaraghavan, N., Adikari, S.: An integrated framework for design thinking and agile methods for digital transformation. In: Marcus, A. (ed.) DUXU 2016. LNCS, vol. 9746, pp. 34–42. Springer, Cham (2016). doi:10.1007/978-3-319-40409-7_4
17. Miller, T., Pedell, S., Lopez-Lorca, A.A., Mendoza, A., Sterling, L., Keirnan, A.: Emotion-led modelling for people-oriented requirements engineering: the case study of emergency systems. J. Syst. Softw. 105, 54–71 (2015)
18. Strauss, A., Corbin, J.: Basics of Qualitative Research Grounded Theory Procedures and Techniques. Sage Publications Inc., Thousand Oaks (1990)
19. Bolling, M., Eriksson, Y.: Collaboration with society: the future role of universities? Identifying challenges evaluation. Res. Eval. 25(2), 209–218 (2016)

Introducing Fundamental Concepts of Process Modeling Through Participatory Simulation

Stefan Oppl[1,2(✉)] and Stijn Hoppenbrouwers[1,3]

[1] Department of Software Science, Radboud University, Toernooiveld 212,
6525 EC Nijmegen, Netherlands
[2] Department of Business Information Systems – Communications Engineering,
Johannes Kepler University Linz, Altenberger Straße 69, 4040 Linz, Austria
stefan.oppl@jku.at
[3] Model-Based IS Group, HAN University of Applied Sciences, Ruitenberglaan 26, 6802 CE
Arnhem, Netherlands
stijn.hoppenbrouwers@han.nl

Abstract. Due to the ubiquitous deployment of information systems in today's organizational work settings, the importance of process modeling skills is undisputed not only for techno-centric roles in organizations, but also for more business-oriented positions. The ability to understand and shape work processes through modeling practices is important to actively contribute to information system design. How to facilitate the development of modeling skills for a non-technology-proficient target group has hardly been subject of research. We aim at addressing this issue with an experiential learning approach using participatory simulations of process models. By letting participants experience work processes and reflect on their underlying structure, we aim at facilitating the development of an abstract conceptual understanding, which can then be validated by actively experimenting with process modifications. In the present paper, we introduce the conceptual foundations of our approach, and describe the interactive system we have developed to facilitate the participatory simulation process. Initial findings from an exploratory study with the system indicate that it can support experiential learning processes.

Keywords: Experiential learning · Interactive process simulation · Business process modeling education

1 Introduction

Process modeling is an important part in the design of modern information systems [1]. With topics like model-based business-IT-alignment gaining more attention recently [2], the question of how to qualify non-IT-proficient stakeholders for actively contributing to modeling activities in IS design is highly relevant [3]. Process modeling traditionally has been considered an experts' discipline, where stakeholders with domain-specific knowledge were solely considered providers of unstructured input, which subsequently had to be translated to sound conceptual process models [4]. The ubiquitous deployment of IS and IT artifacts in daily business operation, which all intervene in or influence

© Springer International Publishing AG 2017
A. Metzger and A. Persson (Eds.): CAiSE 2017 Workshops, LNBIP 286, pp. 110–122, 2017.
DOI: 10.1007/978-3-319-60048-2_11

peoples' alternatives to act in their professional environment, challenges the distinction between (non-modeling) domain experts and (model-creating) system analysts. This challenge is met in research by either providing means for pre-structuring domain expert's inputs in a way that makes it easy to be adopted in information system models (e.g., [5]) or using modeling languages and/or facilitation techniques that are more accessible to domain experts than traditional technology-centric approaches like UML (e.g., [6]). Industry has also recognized the need for such approaches and has reacted with systems that are recently referred to as low-code platforms[1].

While these approaches seem to be successful with respect to the aim of designing information systems that meet the needs and requirements of its prospective users, they do not explicitly address how to support the development of an understanding of modeling concepts and skills in appropriately applying them. Research in areas like end-user development [7] and programming education [8] has explicitly adopted this perspective. It, however, has so far largely been ignored in business and information systems research. This paper makes a first step towards addressing this issue. It introduces an instrument that supports domain experts without modeling experiences to develop an understanding of the relationship between conceptual process models and actual work processes by interactive participatory simulations. Following the experiential learning paradigm, we hypothesize that anchoring the discovery of modeling concepts in the actual work process should enable domain experts to articulate their perceptions about their work in appropriate process modeling constructs. In this paper, we focus on the design of the support instrument that will enable us to examine this hypothesis in future research.

We proceed as follows: First, we revisit approaches on teaching process modeling concepts and support modeling skill development to position our approach in the body of available prior research. We then elaborate on the approach of introducing process modeling concepts through participatory simulations. In the following section, we introduce our proposed support platform. We finally briefly report on our initial experiences when deploying the platform educational settings.

2   Teaching Process Modeling - State-of-the-Art

Process Modeling has been recognized as a teaching challenge as early as the 1960s [9]. Existing research has addressed this challenge largely from a didactical perspective on curriculum- or course-level. In formal, curriculum-based educational settings, teaching process modeling has been a topic of research. It has been examined on a curriculum level by Stewart [10]. Single course designs have been proposed and evaluated in this area [11–13]. All these works, however, focus on content and course organization and largely omit methodological questions that examine how an understanding for process modeling concepts can be developed.

In terms of global methodology, Powell [14] calls for teaching conceptual modeling in a setup that allows to work with prototypes, enabling students to iteratively build and

---

[1] The Forrester Wave: Low-Code Development Platforms, Q2 2016.

assess their models. Recker and Rosemann [11] suggest to take modeling cases from disciplines familiar to students, enabling them to focus on the development of the ability to identify, and critically reflect upon, relevant "process" concepts. Stewart and Rosemann [10] report on successful teaching interventions in information systems education with an inverted curriculum approach, letting students experience modeling in a practice-oriented context first, and only subsequently learn the detailed conceptual foundations.

Regarding operative teaching methodology, Powell and Willemain [15] have empirically examined mathematical modeling processes of novice learners and derive qualitative insights and implications for teaching from their observations: (a) students need to be guided to develop an abstract understanding of a problem from concrete instances of this problem; (b) students require support in progress-monitoring during problem solving, e.g., by pointing them to open issues in their current model version; and (c) prototyping helps in developing increasingly complex and insightful models.

Desel [16] stresses the importance of using interactive simulations to validate behavioral models of systems. Validation through simulation is used as a means of learning about the properties of a model from its simulated behavior and eventually adapt it to meet expected behavior or other desired properties. Interactive simulations incorporate users' activities and allow them to experience the modeled behavior. In the same line—with a focus on socio-technical business systems as a whole—Buur et al. [17] argue for participatory simulations via interactive role playing to validate business models and develop an understanding about fundamental modeling concepts. It is important to stress here, that the simulations proposed in these works focus on behavioral simulations of socio-technical systems under the interactive involvement of users rather than simulations of the input/output behavior of information systems that are considered black boxes.

The review of existing methodological considerations as presented above on how to develop generalizable conceptualizations of ones' perceptions of a work process point at following an experiential learning approach [18] for operatively supporting the learning process. In the context of the present work, this means that an appropriate approach should let learners experience processes, which are represented in conceptual models, and—based on their perceptions—reflect on their underlying structure. Following the experiential learning paradigm, this should start with experiencing the behavior exposed by actors in a work process, facilitate the development of an abstract conceptual understanding, which then in turn should be validated by actively experimenting with process modifications (i.e., iteratively altering the model and experiencing the changed process).

Such experiential learning approaches have been successfully deployed in different disciplines to introduce learners to domain-specific concepts and facilitate the development of their skills in appropriately handling them. Thatcher [19] discusses how experiential learning in general can be facilitated through games and simulation, stressing the importance of such simulations being of participatory nature and accompanying them with a debriefing-phase that is used to reflect on the experiences and conceptual findings of the involved participants. Several researchers have examined participatory simulations to aid the development of abstractions skills: The interactive programming environment Scratch[2] has been successfully deployed to support novices to develop an understanding of fundamental computer science concepts via guided iterative experimentation and modeling activities [8, 20].

Research in the area of end-user development provides evidence that live evaluation via interactive simulation of models supports understanding of the effects a model has on the actual work process [21] or on the software described in the model [22], in particular when the effects of changes made to a model are immediately visible in the simulation [23]. Experiential learning based on simulation has also been deployed in other disciplines, such as industrial management [24] or work system design [25]. Clancey et al. [25] call for simulations based on interaction-oriented modeling rather than flow-oriented modeling to enable a more immediate connection to practicioners' perceptions of their work systems. De Smedt et al. [26] show, how gamified simulation of declarative process models can aid the understanding of the semantics represented in the models.

Summarizing, the reviewed related work in general proposes a practice-oriented introduction of modeling fundamentals, and indicates that interactive simulations can enable linking the behavior represented in a process model to its constitutive elements. Concrete methodology on an operative level or tools support for such learning processes, however, have hardly been a subject of research. We thus examine related disciplines such as programming education in the next section on how interactive simulations can be used methodologically and technically for the aims of the present article.

3   Participatory Simulation Support Instrument

The requirements on an instrument supporting participatory simulation can be derived from the results of our literature review. The state-of-the-art in process modeling education indicates that learning processes on understanding process modeling are supported by anchoring them on actual experiences of the process. The findings on how to support experiential learning processes by interactive model simulation leads us to hypothesize that mapping perceptions of the simulated process and the underlying model can be supported by interactive experimentation with the model. This leads to an indicative list of four requirements on the instrument itself:

- $R1$: Enable experiential learning through participatory interactive simulations of (work) processes in an actor-centric way [8, 25]
- $R2$: Enable to experiment with the simulation and change the underlying model [14, 16, 17], where changes to the underlying model have to be immediately explorable (i.e., without re-starting the simulation) [7, 23]
- $R3$: Provide support for learners using different abstractions of the work process when exploring and/or altering processes to help them understand the link between their perception of the work process and the underlying model [15, 20]

---

[2] https://scratch.mit.edu.

– *R4*: Provide interactive guidance during the phases of experiential learning [15, 24], including ex-post debriefing phases to discuss individual learnings and explicitly reflect on the generic concepts identified during participatory simulation [10, 19].

Based on these requirements, we have designed and implemented an instrument that should support learning about modeling concepts via participatory simulation. It is supported by a web-based platform, which we introduce in the following. The technical design of this platform has been described in [27]. Here, we focus on those features that aim at supporting the development of a conceptual understanding about process modeling.

The instrument is built using the Vaad in framework[3]. It follows an actor-centric approach for simulation processes. The instrument is designed to be used in group settings, where at least one person representing each of the actors modeled in the process should participate. The components of the instrument (cf. Fig. 1) are designed along the requirements identified in the former section.

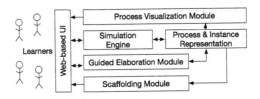

Fig. 1. Architectural overview

The core of the instrument is the *simulation engine*, which enables users to interactively simulate process models and explore their structure in an experiential way (*R1*). Simulation is based on the *process representation*, which is stored in an actor-centric way (*R1*). During simulation, the current progress in the process and its history are represented in an *instance representation*. Process models can be stored in and loaded from an XML-based format for accessing earlier results.

The *guided elaboration module* enables users to alter the process underlying the simulation and continue the simulation immediately at the modified position (*R2*). It does not require users to manipulate the process model directly, but guides them through the elaboration process using prompts that elicit the required information based on the simulation state the elaboration process was triggered in (*R3*).

Simulations of a process can be carried out an arbitrary number of times, where the instrument keeps track of which aspects of the model have not yet been explored (*R2*). The *scaffolding module*, among other features, provides hints at how to progress with the participatory simulation to explore all aspects of the underlying process (*R4*).

The *process visualization module* provides graphical representations of the process model with various complexity that can be used based on the participants' needs and capabilities (*R3*). It is furthermore capable of visualizing the current state of the simulation and the path taken through the process so far (*R4*), as well as the modification

---

[3] https://vaadin.com.

history of the process, which should eventually lead to users recognizing the relationship between modeling constructs and their impact on the activities represented or influenced by them (*R3*). In the following, we describe the different components in more detail.

Process and Instance Representation. The process representation is based on an actor-centric business process modeling approach [28]. The behavioral models of actors are separate processes and are only linked through messages that actors can send and receive. This resembles the semantics of pools and message flows in BPMN. Such loosely coupled processes enable local changes to the model (i.e., only immediately affecting the behavior of one actor).

Elaboration activities can leave the model in an inconsistent state (e.g., an actor could expect a message, which is not yet provided by another actor). Such inconsistencies are kept track of in the process representation and can be resolved later in further elaboration steps.

The instance representation only stores the currently available activities for each actor and the path taken through the process until there (to enable "undo" actions for easier exploration). In a simulation step, the next available activities are always derived directly from the underlying process model. In this way, process changes immediately affect the simulation.

Simulation Engine. The simulation engine uses the data provided by the process and instance representation to render a user interface that enables participatory simulation of the process. It simultaneously displays the current state of each actor and, according to this state, offers interaction options to the participants (cf. Fig. 2).

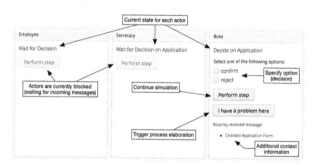

Fig. 2. Simulation interface

This simultaneous visualization of each actor provides a permanent display of the overall context of the current simulation in the participatory setting. Participants thus can track the impact of their interactions with the simulation and in this way learn about the different types of activities (i.e., action, send message, receive message) that constitute the behavioral model of a single actor.

The simulation engine also serves as the gateway to guided elaboration. Process changes are always situated, anchored on the current state of the simulation. In this, way participants can immediately see the impact of their changes on the simulation. They additionally have the option to undo changes if they did not achieve the intended effects. This supports exploratory behavior, strengthening the opportunity to not only explore the process but also gain experience with different types of process changes. In combination with the visualization component described below, this allows to link modeling constructs to experienced simulated behavior during reflection phases, thus further supporting experiential learning.

Scaffolded Exploration. Guidance in the experiential learning process is provided by the scaffolding module. Scaffolding is a concept from the field of educational tutoring [29]. It originally refers to having an experienced person help an unexperienced learner to acquire knowledge about a particular topic. Scaffolding is a metaphor adopted from construction industry and refers to a temporary means of support that is present until the scaffolded entity (here: people acquiring knowledge about process modeling via participatory simulation) can accomplish a given task itself. In order for scaffolds to be acceptable for learning subjects and provide added value to them, they need to be directed appropriately at their current skill level [30]. In the context of the present work, this means that tips on how to explore the simulation need to be provided on different levels of concreteness, depending on the users' proficiency in using the tool.

Figure 3 shows the main scaffolding interface, that allows to navigate through the currently available tips. The mechanism to identify relevant tips has been designed in a flexible way, so that they can target different aspects of the simulation, such as previously unexplored model parts or remaining inconsistencies in the model (for details on which types of tips are relevant, cf. [31]). The right part of Fig. 3 shows a tip on two different levels of concreteness. The tip descriptions are dynamically created based on the current state of the simulation (e.g., the list of required steps in the lower left part of the figure is created based on the currently available activity of the respective actor).

Fig. 3. Interface of scaffolding engine

Guided Elaboration To enable active exploration of different process constructs, guided elaboration is triggered from any currently available activity in the simulation (cf. Fig. 2). The elaboration module renders a user interface that uses dynamically assembled prompts to elicit the information necessary to make the process change as required by the users. Users here are not confronted with modeling constructs, but can specify their changes in a problem-centric way, anchored on the respective activity.

Figure 4 shows a sample prompt for guided elaboration. In this case, the users have chosen that the currently available activity is not appropriate in their current situation, as they would have expected further input to be available before they could execute it.

The prompt shown in Fig. 4 asks them to specify the input they would have expected and where they think they can get it from. The list of further prompts dynamically changes according to their selection, as, e.g., selection of an existing actor as the source of the expected input would not require a further prompt, whereas the current selection leads to the speciation of an additional actor.

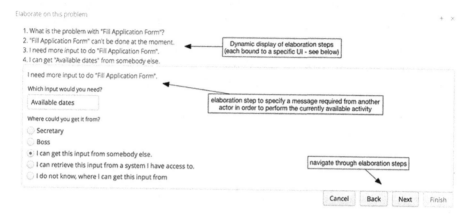

Fig. 4. Interface of elaboration engine

Users are free to navigate through the prompts to explore their options. Once the users confirm their inputs, the changes are applied to the process model. The instance information is adapted, so that users continue the simulation at the modified activity, thus being able to immediately experience the impact of their elaboration. Model changes are stored and can be undone, if the change is recognized to be inappropriate.

Visualization of Models. To enable users to create a link between the current state of the simulation and the underlying model, visualizations of the model can be displayed at any time during exploration. The visualizations are available in different levels of complexity and from different perspectives on the process (view per actor, overall actor-centric view, overall flow-oriented view), and are augmented with information about the current instance, such as the currently available activities and the path through the process. The visualizations are created dynamically using the GraphViz software suite [32].

Figure 5 shows visualizations for an instance that has been simulated halfway through a sample process. The four models at the top of the figure together form the least complex visualization, where the behavior of each actor is shown as a separate model. The model at the very left shows the interaction among the actors. The greyed-out boxes indicate already executed activities, whereas green boxes represent currently available activities. The lower left model in Fig. 5 compiles the separate actor models in a single visualization and enriches them with connections representing the exchanged messages. The lower right model removes the actors as the primary structuring dimension for the overall model and, in this way, provides a flow-oriented view on the process. Users can switch between the actor-specific behavior models, the interaction overview and the two overall views at any point in time and, in this way, can focus on different aspects of the model in the course of simulation or during reflection phases.

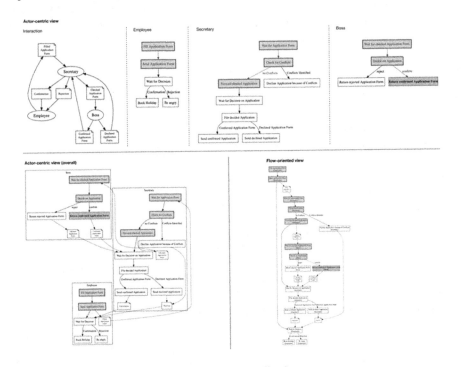

Fig. 5. Process visualizations

4   Exploratory Evaluation

The instrument has been deployed in an exploratory evaluation to perform an initial check of its conformance to the requirements formulated above.

Procedure. The requirements identified in Sect. 3 have been re-formulated to evaluation hypotheses based on their actual implementation in the instrument. They have been examined in an exploratory study. These hypotheses are: *H1*: Experiential learning can be facilitated through participatory simulations of (work) processes in an actor-centric way. *H2a*: The provided instrument facilitates iterative experimentation with the simulation and enables changes to the underlying model. *H2b*: Users understand how to make changes to the model and how to validate them immediately in the simulation. *H3*: Users actively use the different forms of visualization to explore different abstractions of the process. *H4*: The tips provided by the instrument are perceived to be useful in the process of experiential learning.

The hypotheses have been assessed in the study via observation of learners using the instrument and subsequent discussion of their experiences. Observation has been performed by the researchers, who used a semi-structured template for taking notes for each group of learners. Discussion was carried out in the same groups of learners. The discussion was structured along the hypotheses formulated above.

The evaluation was carried out in a course on interactive systems design with 52 students of business information systems in the second or third year of their studies (40 male, 12 female, age ranging between 21 and 45). All participants had initial experiences in business process modeling with BPMN. The participants formed 12 groups of 4–5 participants. They were asked to perform 3 participatory simulations with different tasks. Task design was oriented towards experiential learning, starting with exploratory tasks and progressing to active experimentation (task 1: focus on exploration of a given process model, task 2: focus on elaboration of a given model with prescribed changes, task 3: focus on developing a model from scratch, based on a description of the required target behavior).

Results. We briefly describe our findings from the exploratory study with respect to the hypothesis formulated above.

H1:   The observed behavior throughout all groups indicates that experiential learning about the intended topics took place after an on boarding-phase on using the instrument with varying length. After the participants had explored the instrument and understood its features, they started to reflect on the simulations content-wise and tried to map their observations to process modeling concepts (as they already had fundamental knowledge of BPMN). In the simulations containing elaboration tasks, most groups spent extensive amounts of time thinking about how the prompts of the elaboration guidance module translated to particular model elements. They subsequently confirmed their assumptions using the provided visualizations. Our observations were confirmed in the discussions, where participants frequently stated that they were permanently triggered to think about the underlying model constructs during elaboration. Overall, there are indications that H1 can be confirmed

H2a: The observed behaviors during completing the simulation and elaboration tasks indicate that the instrument was perceived to be largely adequate in supporting experimentation. The users actively explored the provided processes and the elaboration options. The option to undo changes was regularly used, if a change did not achieve the intended effects. The users, however, also encountered limitations in the guided elaboration module that prevented them from performing all their changes as intended (i.e., the prompts did not cover all expected change possibilities). Discussion confirmed that the instrument was perceived to be largely adequate and the provided features were considered useful. Overall, H2a thus can largely be confirmed with some limitations for the current version of the instrument

H2b: Making changes to the underlying model via elaboration initially caused confusion in some groups, as the participants struggled to link the prompts to their intended process modifications. However, after some exploration of the option, the participants were largely able to complete their task. Discussion confirmed that they had no problems in making changes as intended after they had confirmed their initial hypotheses about the link between prompts and inserted model constructs. H2b thus can be partially confirmed for the current version of the instrument

H3:   The visualizations were frequently opened during simulations and used for orientation in the process by all groups. When using visualizations, the participants largely used the models of single actor behaviors, sometimes switching to one of the overall views, if they wanted to explicitly track message exchanges. The actor-centric view was preferred over the flow-oriented view. In the discussion, this preference was attributed to the actor-centric orientation of the simulation interface, which made a mapping of the actor-centric model visualization easier than the flow-oriented visualization. In general, however, the less complex visualizations of the single actor models were preferred. Overall, we could find indications that H3 can be confirmed

H4:   Active use of the exploration and elaboration tips could hardly be observed during the simulation and elaboration tasks. While participants seemed to take notice of the tips, they hardly ever opened the detailed instructions or considered the tips during their activities. During discussion, participants noted that the other elements of the user interface were perceived to be more important and were placed more prominently on the user interface. Furthermore, the ignorance of the tips might also be attributed to the already existing modeling experiences of the participants. Overall, H4 cannot be confirmed for the current version of the instrument

5   Conclusion

In this paper, we have presented an instrument to introduce fundamental process modeling concepts via participatory simulation. The instrument has been designed based on requirements derived from existing research on process modeling education and experiential learning. In an initial exploratory study, we could confirm that the instrument seems to meet the major requirements, but also found some limitations in the modules aiming at supporting the experiential learning process. It needs to be stressed here that the study results are of limited validity due to exploratory nature of the deployed methodology that did not allow to explore potential reasons for observed behavior indepth, but still provide a starting point for further development.

Our future development will initially focus on fixing the limitations identified in the study. The elaboration engine will be refined to cover further possibilities for process changes and eventually also should allow to trigger changes not only from the simulations, but also from model visualizations (to aid the validation of modeling construct hypothesis in later learning phases). Furthermore, introduction of the instrument's features needs to be promoted more actively. In this respect, we currently work on an on boarding system that interactively introduces the features.

On a larger scale, we are planning to embed the instrument's deployment in a whole course design to satisfy the requirement of a debriefing phase. This will allow to study the instrument's effects regarding the aim of supporting learners in acquiring fundamental knowledge about process modeling constructs.

References

1. Fayoumi, A., Loucopoulos, P.: Conceptual modeling for the design of intelligent and emergent information systems. Expert Syst. Appl. **59**, 174–194 (2016)
2. Korhonen, J.J., Kaidalova, J.: Enterprise modeling facilitating business and IT alignment along the social dimension: stakeholder intentions for model-based communication and coordination. In: Proceeding of Business Informatics (CBI) (2015)
3. Recker, J.C., Reijers, H.A., van de Wouw, S.G.: Process model comprehension: the effects of cognitive abilities, learning style, and strategy. CAIS **34**, 199–222 (2014)
4. Frederiks, P.J.M., van der Weide, T.P.: Information modeling: the process and the required competencies of its participants. Data Knowl. Eng. **58**, 4–20 (2006)
5. Front, A., Rieu, D., Santorum, M., Movahedian, F.: A participative end-user method for multi-perspective business process elicitation and improvement. In: SoSyM, pp. 1–24 (2015)
6. Antunes, P., Simões, D., Carriço, L., Pino, J.A.: An end-user approach to business process modeling. J. Network Comput. Appl. **36**, 1466–1479 (2013)
7. Aghaee, S., Pautasso, C.: End-user development of mashups with naturalmash. J. Vis. Lang. Comput. **25**, 414–432 (2014)
8. Dasgupta, S., Resnick, M.: Engaging novices in programming, experimenting, and learning with data. ACM Inroads **5**, 72–75 (2014)
9. Morris, W.T.: On the art of modeling. Manage. Sci. **13**, B-707–B-717 (1967)
10. Stewart, G., Rosemann, M.: Process modeling: a teaching approach for developing generic skills in IT students. In: Proceedings of the 7th ACIS, pp. 20–27 (2001)
11. Recker, J.C., Rosemann, M.: Teaching business process modelling: experiences and recommendations. CAIS **25**, 32 (2009)
12. Ravesteyn, P., Versendaal, J.: Design and implementation of business process management curriculum: a case in dutch higher education. In: Reynolds, N., Turcsányi-Szabó, M. (eds.) KCKS 2010. IFIPAICT, vol. 324, pp. 310–321. Springer, Heidelberg (2010). doi:10.1007/978-3-642-15378-5_30
13. Bider, I., Henkel, M., Kowalski, S., Perjons, E.: Technology enhanced learning of modeling skills in the field of information systems. In: Proceedings of the 8th IADIS (2015)
14. Powell, S.: The teachers' forum: six key modeling heuristics. Interfaces **25**, 114 (1995)
15. Powell, S.G., Willemain, T.R.: How novices formulate models. Part I: qualitative insights and implications for teaching. J. Oper. Res. Soc. **58**, 983–995 (2007)
16. Desel, J.: Teaching system modeling, simulation and validation. In: Proceeding of the 32nd Conference on Winter Simulation (2000)
17. Buur, J., Ankenbrand, B., Mitchell, R.: Participatory business modelling. CoDesign **9**, 55–71 (2013)
18. Kolb, D.A.: Experiential Learning: Experience as the Source of Learning and Development. Prentice Hall, Englewood Cliffs (1984)
19. Thatcher, D.C.: Promoting learning through games and simulations. Simul. Gaming **21**, 262–273 (1990)
20. Meerbaum-Salant, O., Armoni, M., Ben-Ari, M.: Learning computer science concepts with scratch. Comput. Sci. Educ. **23**, 239–264 (2013)
21. Aghaee, S., Pautasso, C., De Angeli, A.: Natural end-user development of web mashups. In: Proceeding of VL/HCC 2013 (2013)
22. Sedrakyan, G., Snoeck, M., Poelmans, S.: Assessing the effectiveness of feedback enabled simulation in teaching conceptual modeling. Comput. Educ. **78**, 367–382 (2014)

23. Repenning, A., Ioannidou, A.: What makes end-user development tick? 13 design guidelines. In: Lieberman, H., Paternò, F., Wulf, V. (eds.) End User Development. HCI, vol. 9, pp. 51–85. Springer, Netherlands (2010). doi:10.1007/1-4020-5386-X_4
24. Smeds, R.: Simulation for accelerated learning and development in industrial management. Prod. Plann. Control **14**, 107–110 (2003)
25. Clancey, W.J., Sachs, P., Sierhuis, M., van Hoof, R.: Brahms: simulating practice for work systems design. Int. J. Hum Comput Stud. **49**, 831–865 (1998)
26. Smedt, J., Weerdt, J., Serral, E., Vanthienen, J.: Gamification of declarative process models for learning and model verification. In: Reichert, M., Reijers, Hajo A. (eds.) BPM 2015. LNBIP, vol. 256, pp. 432–443. Springer, Cham (2016). doi:10.1007/978-3-319-42887-1_35
27. Oppl, S.: Business process elaboration through virtual enactment. In: Proceedings of S-BPM ONE 2017 (2017)
28. Fleischmann, A., Stary, C.: Whom to talk to? A stakeholder perspective on business process development. Univ. Access Inf. Soc. **11**, 125–150 (2012)
29. Wood, D., Bruner, J.S., Ross, G.: The role of tutoring in problem solving. J. Child Psychol. Psychiatry **17**, 89–100 (1976)
30. Dennen, V.P.: Cognitive apprenticeship in educational practice: research on scaffolding, modeling, mentoring, and coaching as instructional strategies. Handbook Res. Educ. Commun. Technol. **2**, 813–828 (2004)
31. Oppl, S., Hoppenbrouwers, S.: Scaffolding Stakeholder-Centric Enterprise Model Articulation. In: The Practice of Enterprise Modeling. pp. 133–147. Springer (2016)
32. Ellson, J., Gansner, E., Koutsofios, L., North, S.C., Woodhull, G.: Graphviz—open source graph drawing tools. In: Presented at the International Symposium on Graph Drawing (2001)

Author Index

Printed in the United States
By Bookmasters